The AMISH BAKING COOKBOOK

GEORGIA VAROZZA & KATHLEEN KERR

HARVEST HOUSE PUBLISHERS
EUGENE, OREGON

All Scripture quotations are from the King James Version of the Bible.

Cover by Dugan Design Group, Bloomington, Minnesota

Cover photo © Dugan Design Group; Cover illustration © weknow / Fotolia

THE AMISH BAKING COOKBOOK
Copyright © 2014 by Georgia Varozza and Kathleen Kerr
Published by Harvest House Publishers
Eugene, Oregon 97408
www.harvesthousepublishers.com

Library of Congress Cataloging-in-Publication Data
Varozza, Georgia
The Amish baking cookbook / Georgia Varozza and Kathleen Kerr.
    pages cm
Includes index.
ISBN 978-0-7369-5538-6 (pbk.)
ISBN 978-0-7369-5539-3 (eBook)
1. Baking. 2. Amish cooking. I. Kerr, Kathleen, II. Title.
TX763.V37 2014
641.5'66—dc23

                                                                2013043569

Printed in China

        19 20 21 22 23 24 25 26 / RDS-JH / 10 9 8 7 6 5 4 3 2

To Martha Edith Stickney and Anne Elizabeth Schmidt,
who taught me to bake hugs and prayers into everything,
and to Carolyn Martha Kerr with anticipation
K.K.

To my beloved crew, in order of appearance—
Walker, Travis, Logan, Sara, Crystalynn,
Audrey, Asher, Easton, and Alexis
G.V.

As for me and my house,
we will serve the LORD.
Joshua 24:15

CONTENTS

WHAT THE AMISH BELIEVE... 7

INTRODUCTION... 11

YEAST BREADS... 13

BAGELS, BUNS, PIZZA CRUSTS,
AND MORE... 45

QUICK BREADS... 69

BISCUITS AND MUFFINS... 87

DOUGHNUTS AND SWEET ROLLS... 105

COOKIES... 137

BARS... 161

CAKES... 187

PIES, COBBLERS, AND CRISPS... 221

INDEX... 263

YEAST BREADS

BAGELS, BUNS, PIZZA CRUSTS...

QUICK BREADS

BISCUITS AND MUFFINS

DOUGHNUTS AND SWEET ROLLS

COOKIES

BARS

CAKES

PIES, COBBLERS, AND CRISPS

WHAT THE AMISH BELIEVE

The Swiss Brethren were a group of faithful men and women who broke from the Catholic and Protestant state churches during the Protestant Reformation in 1525. Derisively called *Anabaptists,* meaning "rebaptizers," many were hunted down and martyred for their beliefs, beginning in 1527 with the public execution of Felix Manz. To escape this persecution, they migrated from Switzerland to Alsace (now part of France), and there they experienced a division in 1693. Bishop Jacob Ammann (from whom the Amish derive their group name) felt the people were becoming lax and called for stricter rules, including shunning (the practice by which a person who falls into sin is banned from associating with baptized believers in any way until such time as he or she publicly repents and is accepted back into the fold). The followers who did not believe in shunning became known as *Mennonites* (so named after the Dutch bishop Menno Simons).

During the 1700s, the Amish were forced to relocate many times due to unsympathetic rulers. In about 1727, the first Amish immigrants arrived in America, and during the 1800s, immigration increased. A number of communities sprang up in America as well as in Canada. Today there are no Amish communities left in Europe, but in North America, Amish congregations flourish. The Amish prefer a rural existence and retain many old customs—thus the use of horse and buggy for transportation, their distinctive dress, and large gardens that help to feed their families.

They are also well versed in the Scripture verses that help to define their faith:

- *Nonconformity and separation of church and state:* "Be not conformed to this world: but be ye transformed by the renewing of your mind, that ye may prove what is that good, and acceptable, and perfect, will of God" (Romans 12:2). And also, "Come out from among them, and be ye separate, saith the Lord" (2 Corinthians 6:17).

- *Nonresistance and refusal to serve in the military:* "But I say unto you, That ye resist not evil: but whosoever shall smite thee on thy right cheek, turn to him the other also" (Matthew 5:39). And also, "If it be possible, as much as lieth in you, live peaceably with all men" (Romans 12:18).

- *No photos of faces:* Thou shalt not make unto thee any graven image, or any likeness of any thing that is in heaven above, or that is in the earth beneath, or that is in the water under the earth (Exodus 20:4).

- *Mutual aid and refusal of insurance or Social Security benefits:* "But if any provide not for his own, and specially for those of his own house, he hath denied the faith, and is worse than an infidel" (1 Timothy 5:8).

- *Rejection of oaths:* "But I say unto you, Swear not at all; neither by heaven; for it is God's throne...But let your communication be, Yea, yea; Nay, nay: for whatsoever is more than these cometh of evil" (Matthew 5:34, 37).

- *Prayer coverings:* "But every woman that prayeth or prophesieth with her head uncovered dishonoureth her head" (1 Corinthians 11:5).

- *House church:* "God that made the world and all things therein, seeing that he is Lord of heaven and earth, dwelleth not in temples made with hands" (Acts 17:24).

- *Adult baptism:* "Jesus answered, Verily, verily, I say unto thee, Except a man be born of water and of the Spirit, he cannot enter into the kingdom of God" (John 3:5).

Despite our modern proclivity for moving around and assimilating into the broader culture, the Amish and Mennonites, on the other hand, have been able to maintain their distinct group identity. Their growth is robust, and they cling to their way of life. They do make changes to their rules and traditions over the years, but they go about it in a slow and thoughtful manner. Their overarching desire as they interact with the broader society is to "lead a quiet and peaceable life in all godliness and honesty" (1 Timothy 2:2).

INTRODUCTION

There's probably nothing that speaks to the comforts of home quite like the yeasty aroma of just-baked bread, the sweet richness of fresh-from-the-oven cookies, or the tart and fruity goodness of a well-made pie. It wasn't that many years ago that if you desired a sweet treat, you made it from scratch. And with so many folks living in rural areas, the ingredients for a baked treat were in ample supply—grain to grind into flour came from the surrounding fields; milk, cream, and butter came from the cows in the barn; and eggs were gathered fresh daily from the flock of chickens just steps from the farmhouse back door. But as more and more people moved off the farms and into the cities, cooking habits changed. For many folks, it became convenient to run down to the local grocery and buy food already made, boxed, and ready to go. But there were holdouts—women (and some men!) who *enjoyed* baking for their loved ones and refused to go the way of modernity.

My mother was one such woman. Every day she fed seven people three hearty and nutritious meals—and not one was made from processed food. It was always homemade from scratch. Sunday was our big food day, and dinner was always more elaborate than our weekday fare. Best of all were the Sunday desserts. This was the day Mama reserved for such delicacies as layer cakes, pies of all kinds, or deep-fried doughnuts or fattigman.

I have fond memories of coming home from school in the afternoons to my mother's greeting, cheerful smile, and some kind of freshly baked treat warm from the oven. Oh, the delicious smells that emanated from our kitchen! Most often she made cookies, but part of the fun was guessing, with only our noses to guide us, what was in store for our afternoon snack. Mama would pour each of us a tall glass of milk and then encourage us to eat up and "take the edge off until dinner." We didn't need to be asked twice!

We hope you enjoy these recipes. There is much to choose from. Some of the recipes are quick and easy to prepare while others require more time and patience. But all of them are great tasting. Make something special for your family today. Enjoy that moment when your loved ones' eyes light up with gladness when they see what you have made with your hands and served from your heart.

Georgia Varozza
Kathleen Kerr

YEAST BREADS

Baking a moist, beautifully textured loaf of bread is the quintessential homemaking skill for Amish women and non-Amish alike. There is nothing to compare to the experience of taking your first bite of warm, homemade bread fresh from the oven. In our house, the heels are greatly coveted—we consider them chewy, fragrant, buttered bliss. And since I usually make at least 4 loaves at a time, all of us are able to indulge. The only thing better than a fresh-from-the-oven bread heel is a loaf of fresh-from-the-oven cinnamon bread. When *that* loaf exits the oven, we all just stand around and tuck away piece after piece until it is completely gone.

In this chapter, you'll find plenty of recipes that you can follow from start to finish, but first we'll cover the various ingredients that go into a good loaf of bread. Then we'll explain the process used to knead, raise, and bake the perfect loaf—because probably more than any other type of food, a loaf of bread is no better than the ingredients that go into it and the care given in the preparation thereof.

Flour

Flour is the main ingredient in bread, and there are many different types you can use. Depending on your choice, you can radically alter the taste and texture of your finished loaf.

Freshly ground *whole flours* have a more robust flavor and more vitamins because none of the grain parts have been removed. However, the oily germ found in whole flours will turn rancid fairly quickly, so buy or grind only small quantities and store the flour in an airtight container in a cool, dark place or in the freezer. But remember! If your flour stays in the freezer, give it plenty of time to come to room temperature before using so the action of the yeast isn't inhibited by the cool temperature.

All-purpose white flour is used in most recipes. All-purpose flour produces a more delicate flavor and texture than whole grain flours, and it is higher in gluten—a protein substance that gives bread dough that elastic quality and traps the air bubbles yeast creates. For this reason, the finished bread will be lighter in texture. But because the bran and germ have been removed, white flour is less nutritious and loses the rich brown color of whole wheat flour.

Bread flour is made from hard red or white wheat berries, which have a higher protein content. If you decide to grind your own flour for bread baking, use hard white or red winter wheat. It's the benchmark for a good loaf of bread. (The soft spring wheat doesn't contain enough gluten to hold the bread loaf together while rising and baking. Instead, use soft wheat for making cookies, cakes, muffins, and the like.)

Other flours and cereals, such as rye, oat, barley, cornmeal, buckwheat, and rice, can be added for extra nutrition as well as taste. Try adding a handful of oatmeal or grind a small amount of buckwheat for additional nutrition and flavor. The possibilities are many.

Vital wheat gluten is considered…well, *vital* when making bread with all whole wheat or rye flour or bread that includes lots of nuts and seeds. Adding gluten improves the dough's elasticity and helps your bread rise. It also makes the finished product better textured and chewy. A little vital wheat gluten goes a long way. You need to use only one tablespoon for every three cups of flour. Even though it's not technically flour, it is sometimes sold as "Vital

Wheat Gluten Flour," so don't let that confuse you. And let me just say that I rarely use vital wheat gluten because I think it's expensive and I have fine luck without it. I'll admit that my bread might be a tad more refined when I add vital wheat gluten, but we've been eating my bread for many years without it, and no one seems to mind a bit. But suit yourself.

Cornell University's Triple-Rich Protein Formula

In the 1930s, Dr. Clive McCay, a professor at Cornell University, developed the following formula for adding extra protein to homemade bread. You can use this formula in either white or wheat bread, and the flavor of your finished product will actually be enhanced. For every cup measure of flour, first put the following into the bottom of the cup:

1 T. soy flour
1 T. dry milk powder
1 tsp. wheat germ

Yeast

Yeast is actually a living organism. It's the all-important rising agent in bread baking. Yeast comes in these forms: active dry, fresh or compressed cakes, or instant or quick-rising. Use *active dry yeast* for your baking needs. You can buy it in individual-use packets or in bulk, which costs considerably less. Once the package is opened, store yeast in the refrigerator. Properly stored, yeast can last up to two years.

To activate and verify that your yeast is still fresh, bring it to room temperature. Then add it to warm liquid (about 110°) with a pinch of sugar. Leave the mixture for about ten minutes. If all is well, the mixture will bubble and look creamy on the top. This step is called "proofing the yeast."

Yeast can be killed by heat, so it's better if the liquid is a bit too cool than too warm. If it's activated in a slightly cool liquid, the yeast will just take longer to bubble. But if you add it to too-hot water, the yeast will die and be of no use.

Liquid

You can use water or milk or a combination of the two. It's also possible to use buttermilk, potato water, sour milk, or cream for your liquid. Water makes your finished bread chewier and somewhat coarser in the grain. Milk produces a tenderer, finer grained, cakelike loaf.

Fat

Most bread recipes call for a small amount of fat, which can be added in the form of vegetable oil, butter, lard, or shortening to make your bread lighter, finer grained, and tenderer.

Sweeteners and Salt

Sweeteners in the form of sugar, honey, agave syrup, molasses, or sorghum are used to promote rising and add flavor. Honey helps bread stay fresh longer and is a great choice.

Salt is actually a yeast inhibitor, but it is used in such a small quantity that it's not a problem. It's a good idea to use a bit more salt in your recipes on especially warm days so your bread doesn't rise too quickly, which could lead to large air pockets or a fallen loaf. Plus, as in most recipes, a small amount of salt seems to bring out the flavor of the other ingredients—your bread will just plain taste better.

Nuts and Seeds

Nuts and seeds are a good addition to your bread. Some of the more common nuts and seeds used in bread are chopped walnuts, pecans, and pine nuts, and sunflower, poppy, sesame, flax, and chia seeds. You can also sprout seeds, legumes, or grains (including wheat!) such as alfalfa, millet, barley, lentils, or soy to add to your bread.

General Bread Making Hints—Kneading and Rising

Although recipes vary and call for different ingredients, procedures, and baking temperatures and times, most of the time you will follow these simple instructions to turn out satisfying and successful breads and rolls.

After mixing the recipe ingredients, turn out the lump of dough onto a clean and floured surface, such as your kitchen counter. The dough will be quite sticky, especially at first, so it's a good idea to grease your hands with shortening or butter and re-grease them as needed while you knead the dough. Alternatively, flour your hands instead of greasing them to prevent the dough from sticking to you. This works better for me, but I know some experienced bread bakers who swear by greased palms, so experiment and decide what works best for you.

As you knead the dough, keep adding flour to the work surface so the dough doesn't stick, but try to use as little as possible. You might end up using as much as a cup of flour during the kneading process, depending on how many loaves you are kneading. This is fine as long as your dough isn't too dry.

To knead, fold the dough slightly less than in half toward you and then press the dough down as you push it away from you. Turn the dough a quarter turn and again fold it slightly less than in half toward you, and press down and away. Continue turning, folding, and pressing. Use a smooth, steady, rhythmic pattern, and continue kneading for five to ten minutes. Generally, hearty bread recipes require a longer kneading period, while lighter sweet breads and rolls need less time.

When you are through kneading the dough, place it in a large, greased bowl with plenty of room for the dough to double in size. Lightly grease the entire surface of the dough ball, cover the bowl with a towel, and set it in a warm (but not too warm), draft-free place. Let it rise until double. I generally place my bowl of dough on the kitchen counter, but if it's especially cold in your home, try to find a slightly warmer spot, such as near a heater vent (but not too near!) or on top of the refrigerator. Although the dough usually takes just an hour to double in size, the time can vary from half an hour to up to two hours. You can tell if the dough has doubled by pressing a finger into the top of the dough. If the indentation stays, it's ready. Keep in mind that a quick rise isn't necessarily the best—slower rising bread dough seems to make the finished product finer textured. When the rise is complete, punch down the dough by giving the top of the loaf a good whack with your knuckles. The dough will fall as the air is released.

Now turn the dough out once again onto your clean surface and gently knead it for about a minute. Place the dough back into the greased bowl, re-grease the entire surface of the dough ball, cover it with a towel, and let it rise again until double. The second rising usually takes less time than the first rising. At this point, you can either loaf it up and place it into the pan (see below), or you can let it rise one more time. I find that allowing the dough to rise twice in the bowl and then again in the pan is enough to produce a nicely textured bread, but there have been times when I've been so pressed for time that I've let the dough rise just once before loafing it up and setting it to rise in the pan. The bread won't be as fine in texture, but at least there's bread for dinner.

Grease your bread pan thoroughly. If you are making more than one loaf, divide the dough into equal portions and form them into loaves. If you have any folds or seams, pinch them well and put those toward the bottom of the pan so the top of the bread is smooth. Before you drop the dough into the pan, give each loaf a few good whacks with the flat of your hand to help pop bubbles. Grease the top of the loaf (not absolutely necessary, by the way, but doing this makes a nice crust) and then prick it several times with a fork. Cover the pan with a towel and set it back in that warm, draft-free place to rise until almost doubled—about an inch above the top of the pan—because the bread will continue to rise about another inch after you put it in the oven to bake. If the dough rises too high before baking, it could collapse while in the oven. (Even if the loaf collapses and does not win a prize, it will still taste fine, albeit dense. Live and learn.)

After you have baked the bread according to the directions for your specific recipe, remove the pan from the oven and immediately put a thin layer of butter or shortening on the top (again, not absolutely necessary). Remove the bread from the pan and cool it on a wire rack. If you store the bread in a plastic bag before it is entirely cool, the crust will stay softer. Try it both ways because you might prefer a stiffer crust.

Remember that homemade bread doesn't keep as long as store-bought, and it will go stale and crumbly quicker too. If you don't eat the loaf before it goes stale, try this. Cube the remaining bread and dry it in a very slow oven (at about 250°). Stir the bread cubes every 15 minutes to evenly dry all sides. You can use the cubes for bread stuffing or croutons or crumble them to sprinkle on top of casseroles and as filler for meatloaf and meatballs. Frankly, that just doesn't happen in my household, so occasionally I'll make four loaves of white bread for the express purpose of making dried bread cubes.

That's it—a perfect loaf of bread!

Basic Per Loaf Bread

For each loaf you wish to make, use the following measurements:

1 cup warm water, about 110° (or use half water and half milk)
1 tsp. melted shortening, butter, or vegetable oil
1 scant tsp. salt
1 T. sugar, honey, or other sweetener of choice
1 tsp. active dry yeast (for 4 loaves, use 1 rounded tablespoon)
3 cups flour

In a mixing bowl, stir together the water, melted shortening, salt, and sugar. Sprinkle the yeast over the top of the mixture and let it stand until the yeast dissolves and starts bubbling a bit, about 10 minutes.

Stir in half of the total amount of flour you plan on using (for instance, 1½ cups flour for each loaf) and beat until smooth. You can use an electric mixer for this part if desired, but you can also mix by hand using a large wooden spoon. Add enough of the remaining flour to make a dough ball that holds together and comes away from the sides of the bowl.

Place the dough onto a floured work surface and knead well for 5 to 10 minutes, adding more flour as needed to keep the dough from sticking.

Put the dough into a large greased bowl and grease all the surfaces of the dough as well. Cover with a towel and let rise until double. Punch down and then lightly knead the dough for a minute or so, grease all surfaces once again, and let it rise in the greased bowl a second time until double. Punch down the dough and form into a loaf. Place the loaf seam-side down into a greased pan and let it rise until almost double.

Preheat oven to 400°. Place the loaf in the preheated oven and then turn the heat down to 350°. Bake about 30 minutes or until done. Remove the loaf from the oven, grease the top if desired, take it out of the baking pan, and cool on a wire rack.

Basic White Bread

2¼ tsp. (1 package) active dry yeast
2 cups warm water
1 T. sugar
6 cups all-purpose flour, approximately
1½ tsp. salt
2 T. softened butter

In a large mixing bowl, combine the yeast, water, and sugar. Let stand about 10 minutes or until bubbly.

Combine 2 cups flour and the salt, add the yeast mixture, and beat at low speed. Add the butter and beat on high speed for 3 minutes. Add ½ cup flour and beat another 4 minutes.

Stir in another 2 to 3 cups flour or enough to make a soft dough. Turn dough out onto a floured surface and knead for 8 to 10 minutes or until dough is smooth and elastic, adding just enough flour to make it workable.

Place dough in a large, buttered or oiled bowl, turning dough so all sides are greased. Cover with a clean towel and let rise until double, about an hour.

Punch down and knead again, then tear dough in half to make 2 balls of dough. Form each half into a loaf and place seam-side down into a greased pan. Cover and let rise in a warm place until double, about 45 minutes.

Bake at 400° for 25 to 30 minutes or until bread is done. Remove from oven and turn out onto a wire rack to cool. Immediately brush tops with melted butter if desired.

- -

Black Bread

2¼ tsp. (1 package) active dry yeast
1⅓ cups strong brewed coffee, room temperature
¼ cup molasses
1 cup whole wheat flour
1 cup rye flour
2 cups all-purpose flour
2 T. unsweetened cocoa powder
1½ tsp. salt
¼ cup vegetable oil
2 T. brown sugar

Mix together yeast, coffee, and molasses. Let set until the yeast is dissolved and the mixture begins to bubble and rise.

In a large bowl, mix together the dry ingredients. Set aside for now.

In another large bowl, stir together the vegetable oil and brown sugar. When the yeast mixture has begun to bubble, add it to the oil and brown sugar mixture and stir well. With a large wooden spoon, add the mixed dry ingredients a bit at a time and beat vigorously after each addition. When the dough pulls away from the sides of the bowl, turn it out onto a floured surface and knead well for 8 to 10 minutes, continuing to add flour as needed so the dough doesn't stick.

Grease a large bowl and place the ball of dough into the bowl, turning the dough so all surfaces are greased. Cover with a towel and let rise until double.

Punch down the dough and knead gently for several minutes. Place the dough back into the greased bowl, turning the dough so all surfaces are again greased. Cover the bowl with a clean towel and let the dough rise a second time until double.

Pat the dough into a ball and place on a greased cookie sheet. Let rise until double and then bake at 375° for 35 to 45 minutes or until done.

Cheddar Cheese Bread

2 T. sugar
2 tsp. salt
4½ tsp. (2 packages) yeast
5 cups all-purpose flour
2¼ cups milk
1 cup shredded Cheddar cheese
1 T. butter, melted

In a large mixing bowl, mix together the sugar, salt, yeast, and 2 cups of the flour.

In a medium saucepan over low heat, heat the milk and cheese until warm, about 120°. (It's fine if the cheese does not entirely melt.)

Using an electric mixer set on low speed, beat the liquid mixture into the flour mixture until blended. Increase the speed to medium and beat for 2 minutes. Beat in 1 more cup of flour and continue beating for 2 minutes. Using a large wooden spoon, gradually stir in enough additional flour to make a stiff dough that pulls away from the sides of the bowl. Cover the dough with a towel and let rise in a warm place until double, about 1 hour.

Stir or punch down dough, form into a round loaf, and place into a greased 2-quart round, shallow casserole dish. Cover and let rise again until double, about 1 hour.

Preheat oven to 375°. Brush loaf with melted butter and bake 30 to 35 minutes or until done. Remove from pan and cool on a wire rack.

Cinnamon Raisin Bread

2 cups buttermilk, heated to very warm
2 T. light brown sugar
3 T. butter
2 tsp. salt
2¼ tsp. (1 package) active dry yeast
¼ cup warm water
½ tsp. sugar
2 tsp. cinnamon
4½ to 5 cups all-purpose flour
1¼ cups raisins, lightly mixed with a small amount of
    flour to help them "float" in the dough
small amount of milk for brushing tops

In a large bowl, mix together the warm buttermilk, brown sugar, butter, and salt.

In a small bowl, stir together the yeast, warm water, and sugar. Let set until the yeast dissolves and the mixture begins to bubble and rise and then add it to the buttermilk mixture.

Stir the cinnamon into 2 cups of the flour and then beat the cinnamon and flour into the buttermilk mixture with an electric mixer on low speed for 1 minute, or beat by hand with a large wooden spoon for 300 strokes.

Stir in the lightly floured raisins and enough of the remaining flour to make the dough ball up and leave the sides of the bowl.

Turn dough out onto a floured surface and knead for 8 to 10 minutes. Grease a bowl and place the dough ball into the bowl, turning the dough so all surfaces are greased as well. Cover the bowl with a towel and let rise until double.

Punch down dough. Knead again for 8 to 10 minutes and then return it to the greased bowl. Let it rest for 20 minutes. Divide dough into 2 loaves and place in greased pans. Cover with a towel and let rise until nearly double.

Brush tops of loaves with milk and bake at 375° for 10 minutes. Reduce heat to 350° and continue baking for another 35 to 40 minutes or until done.

Dilly Rye Bread

1⅓ cups warm water
2 tsp. sugar
1 T. (most of 2 packages) active dry yeast
1½ cups wheat flour
1½ cups rye flour
½ cup vital wheat gluten flour
2 tsp. salt
1 T. dill weed
1 T. dill seed
2 T. molasses
2 T. oil
cornmeal for dusting
1 egg yolk

In a small bowl, mix together the water, sugar, and yeast. Let set until it begins to bubble and froth, about 10 minutes.

In a large mixing bowl, stir together the flours, salt, dill weed, and dill seed. Add the yeast mixture, molasses, and oil and mix with a large wooden spoon until the dough forms. Knead the dough right in the mixing bowl for 10 minutes. Do not add more flour. Although the dough will get sticky and be rather difficult to work, keep kneading.

Ball up the dough and place it in another large bowl that has been greased or oiled. Roll the dough around in the bowl until the entire surface has been greased. Cover the bowl with a towel or plastic wrap and let the dough rise for 1½ to 2 hours.

At the end of the rising time, punch down the dough and knead it in the bowl again for 10 minutes. Cover the bowl and let the dough rest for 15 minutes.

While the dough is resting, grease or oil a baking sheet and sprinkle it with cornmeal.

Divide the dough in half and knead each half separately for 2 minutes. Form each half into an oval or round loaf and put them both on the prepared baking sheet. Beat the egg yolk with 1 teaspoon water and brush the tops of the loaves. With a very sharp knife, make 3 shallow slashes across the top of each loaf. Cover the loaves with a towel or plastic wrap and let rise until double, about 1½ to 2 hours.

Place an ovenproof pan of boiling water on the bottom rack of the oven and preheat oven to 375°. Bake the loaves for 20 to 25 minutes or until done. Cool bread on a wire rack.

Egg Bread

1½ cups scalded milk
½ cup butter
½ cup sugar
4½ tsp. (2 packages) active dry yeast
½ cup warm water
½ tsp. sugar
2 eggs, beaten
9 cups all-purpose flour, more or less
2 tsp. salt

In a large mixing bowl, pour scalded milk over butter and sugar and set aside to cool.

In a small bowl, dissolve yeast in warm water with ½ teaspoon sugar and let stand for 5 minutes.

Add the yeast mixture to the milk mixture and stir. Alternately add the eggs and 3 cups flour. Then add the salt and beat for 3 minutes. By hand, continue adding the rest of the flour and knead until the dough is light and elastic, about 8 minutes. Place the dough in a greased bowl and turn so all sides are covered. Cover and let rise until double.

Shape dough into 3 loaves and place in greased loaf pans. Let rise again for about 20 minutes.

Bake at 425° for 10 minutes, then turn the temperature down to 350° and continue baking for about 30 minutes longer or until done.

French Bread

Note: French bread can't be hurried. The ingredients are minimal, but it's the process that gives French bread its spectacular taste and texture. For a special addition to dinner, start this bread early in the day. And do plan to eat it all in one sitting—French bread doesn't store well.

1 T. active dry yeast (you can use 1 package if that's all you have, but it's better to measure this accurately)
¼ cup warm water
½ tsp. sugar
2 cups lukewarm water
2 tsp. salt
6 cups all-purpose flour
small amount of cornmeal

In a small bowl, mix together the yeast, ¼ cup warm water, and sugar. Let set until the yeast is dissolved and the mixture is beginning to bubble and rise.

In a large bowl, mix together the 2 cups warm water and salt. Add the dissolved yeast mixture and stir well. Using an electric mixer, add 2 cups flour and beat on low speed for 1 minute. Increase speed to medium and beat for another 2 minutes. Scrape the sides of the bowl regularly to get all the bits of flour into the batter.

By hand, stir in enough of the remaining flour to make a ball of dough that pulls away from the sides of the bowl. It will be very soft and sticky.

If the dough seems too sticky to successfully turn out and knead, keep it in the bowl for now and knead the dough with a large wooden spoon or paddle, adding small amounts of flour as you work. After kneading the dough for several minutes, the dough will not be as sticky, and you can then turn the dough ball out onto a well-floured surface or on a floured pastry cloth. The dough will still be sticky, but do your best to work around that.

Knead the dough for about 8 minutes or until it is shiny, elastic, and has air bubbles under the surface. Don't rush this step. Place the dough ball in a very large greased bowl and turn the ball of dough so all surfaces are greased. Cover the bowl with a clean towel and let the dough rise until it's tripled in volume. This will take about 3 hours. You don't want to hurry the rise time because the slow rising will enhance the flavor and texture of the finished loaves.

After the dough has risen, turn it out again on a floured surface and gently knead for several minutes to get out all the air bubbles—use a toothpick if necessary. Place the dough back in the greased bowl, turning the dough to again grease the surfaces, and let it rise a second time until it is slightly more than double. This second rising will take less time, but it will still take at least an hour.

Turn out the dough once more onto the floured surface and gently knead for 2 minutes, making sure to prick the bubbles with a toothpick. Using your hands, flatten the dough into a rectangle and cut into 3 equal portions. Cover them with a towel and let rest for 15 minutes. Then form each portion into a long, narrow loaf by rolling the dough back and forth with your hands and pricking out air bubbles with a toothpick. Make the loaves almost as long as the cookie sheet you will use for baking.

Grease a large cookie sheet and then liberally sprinkle cornmeal on it. Carefully lay the loaves on the cookie sheet, cover with a towel, and let rise again until almost tripled in bulk, about 45 to 60 minutes.

Place a shallow pan of boiling water on the floor of the oven and preheat the oven to 400°. Just before baking, diagonally slash the tops of the loaves in several places using a very sharp knife, and then mist or brush the loaves with cold water. You can also sprinkle on sesame or poppy seeds if desired.

Bake 25 to 35 minutes or until done, misting the bread occasionally while it bakes.

German Dark Rye Bread

3 cups all-purpose flour
4½ tsp. (2 packages) active dry yeast
¼ cup cocoa powder
1 T. caraway seeds
2 cups water
⅓ cup molasses
2 T. butter
1 T. sugar
1 T. salt
3 to 3½ cups rye flour

In a large mixing bowl, combine all-purpose flour, yeast, cocoa powder, and caraway seeds until well blended.

In a saucepan, combine the water, molasses, butter, sugar, and salt. Heat until just warm, stirring occasionally to melt the butter. Add to dry mixture. Beat at low speed for 30 seconds and then at medium for 3 minutes more.

By hand, stir in enough rye flour to make a soft dough. Turn out onto a floured surface and knead until smooth, adding more rye flour as needed, about 8 minutes. Cover and let stand for 20 minutes.

Punch down and divide dough in half. Shape each half into a round loaf and place on greased baking sheets or 2 greased pie plates. Brush surface of loaves with a little vegetable oil. Slash tops of loaves with a sharp knife. Cover with a towel and let rise until double, about 1½ hours.

Bake at 400° for 25 to 30 minutes or until bread looks done. Remove from baking pans and cool on wire racks.

Honey Oatmeal Bread

1 cup boiling water
1 cup rolled oats, uncooked
⅓ cup shortening, softened
⅓ cup honey
1 T. salt
4½ tsp. (2 packages) active dry yeast
1 cup warm water
1 egg
4 to 5 cups whole wheat flour
1 T. melted butter

Stir the boiling water, oats, shortening, honey, and salt together in a large mixing bowl. Cool to lukewarm.

Dissolve yeast into warm water.

Add dissolved yeast mixture, egg, and 2 cups flour to the first mixture. Beat 2 minutes at medium speed or by hand until batter is smooth. By hand, gradually stir in the remaining flour to make a stiff batter. Spread the batter evenly into 2 greased loaf pans. Smooth tops of loaves by patting into shape. Cover and let rise in a warm place for about 1½ hours. Bake at 375° for 50 to 55 minutes. Remove bread from pans and brush tops with melted butter.

Oatmeal Bread

2 cups milk
2 cups rolled oats, uncooked
¼ cup brown sugar, packed
2 T. shortening
1 T. salt
2¼ tsp. (1 package) active dry yeast
½ cup warm water
5 cups all-purpose flour, more or less
egg white (see directions)
1 T. water
small amount rolled oats

Scald milk. Stir in oats, brown sugar, shortening, and salt. Remove from heat and cool to lukewarm.

In a large mixing bowl, sprinkle yeast on warm water and stir to dissolve. Add milk mixture and 2 cups flour. Beat with a spoon until batter is smooth. Add enough remaining flour, a little at a time, until dough becomes soft and leaves the sides of the bowl. Turn onto a floured surface and knead until dough is smooth and elastic, about 8 minutes.

Place the dough ball in a lightly greased bowl. Turn dough so it's greased on all sides. Cover with a clean towel and let stand in a warm place until double, about 1 hour. Punch down and let rise again until nearly double, about 30 minutes.

Turn out onto a lightly floured surface and divide in half to make 2 balls. Cover and let rest for 10 minutes. Shape into loaves and place in 2 greased loaf pans. Let rise again until almost double, about 1 hour. Brush the top of the loaves with egg white beaten with 1 tablespoon water (optional). Sprinkle top with rolled oats.

Bake at 375° for 40 minutes or until done. If bread starts getting too brown, cover loosely with aluminum foil after at least 15 minutes of baking time.

Peasant Bread

2¼ tsp. (1 package) active dry yeast
1 T. sugar
2 tsp. salt
2 cups warm water
1 T. oil plus more for brushing top of loaf (olive oil is a
  good choice in this recipe)
4½ cups all-purpose flour

Mix together the yeast, sugar, and salt. Add the warm water, mix well, and then add the oil. Begin adding the flour a little at a time, incorporating well after each addition. Knead the dough until smooth, about 5 to 7 minutes. Place dough into a greased bowl and cover. Let rise for 30 minutes.

Form into a round loaf and place on a greased cookie sheet. Cover and let rise again, about 45 minutes.

Brush top of loaf with oil and bake in a preheated 425° oven 10 minutes. Reduce the heat to 375°, brush again with oil, and continue baking for 20 more minutes.

Potato Bread

1 medium potato
1 qt. water
2 T. butter
2 tsp. salt
4½ tsp. (2 packages) active dry yeast
1 tsp. sugar
1 cup warm water
11 to 12 cups all-purpose flour

Peel, dice, and boil the potato in the quart of water until tender. Drain the potato, reserving the potato water. Mash the potato well. Add the mashed potato back into the reserved potato water and stir in the butter and salt. Let mixture cool until lukewarm.

Dissolve yeast and sugar in the 1 cup warm water and let stand for about 10 minutes or until the yeast begins to bubble and rise.

In a large bowl, gradually add 6 cups flour to the potato water and beat until smooth. Mix in the dissolved yeast and water mixture and beat thoroughly. Cover the batter with a towel and let rise in a draft-free place for about 2 hours. Then work in enough of the remaining flour to make a soft dough.

Turn out the dough onto a floured surface and knead the dough for about 8 to 10 minutes. Put it into a greased bowl, greasing the dough as well. Cover and let rise until double. Punch down dough and divide into 3 loaves. Place the loaves into 3 greased loaf pans. Cover and let rise until almost double.

Bake at 375° for about 40 minutes or until done.

Raisin Oatmeal Bread

2¼ tsp. (1 package) active dry yeast
2 cups warm water
1½ tsp. salt
3 T. sugar
2 T. shortening
1 cup rolled oats
2 cups all-purpose flour
2 cups whole wheat flour
½ cup seedless raisins

In a large bowl, dissolve the yeast in the warm water. Stir in the salt, sugar, shortening, and rolled oats, plus 2 cups all-purpose flour. Beat mixture for 3 minutes and then stir in the whole wheat flour and the raisins, mixing until the batter is smooth and satiny. Cover with a towel and let rise in a warm place until double.

Stir down batter while slowly counting to 15 and then spoon the batter into 2 greased loaf pans. Cover with a towel and let rise to the top of the pan.

Bake at 350° for 50 minutes.

Round Rye Bread

4 cups all-purpose flour
2 cups rye flour
4½ tsp. (2 packages) yeast
1½ tsp. salt
2 T. caraway seed
2 cups buttermilk
1/3 cup molasses
⅓ cup butter
2 T. melted butter

In a medium bowl, mix together the flour and rye flour. In a large mixing bowl, combine 2 cups of the mixed flour, yeast, salt, and caraway seed.

Heat the buttermilk, molasses, and ⅓ cup butter in a saucepan over low heat until warm (about 120°). The butter won't be entirely melted, and the mixture may look curdled, which is okay. Pour the liquid into the large mixing bowl that contains the flour and yeast mixture. Beat on low speed until blended and then beat on medium speed for 2 minutes. Add another ½ cup of the flour mixture and continue beating for 2 minutes more. With a large wooden spoon, stir in enough additional flour to make a soft dough.

Turn dough out onto a well-floured surface and knead for 10 minutes. Shape dough into a ball and place in a large greased bowl, turning dough so entire surface is greased. Cover with a towel and let rise until double, about 1 to 1½ hours.

Punch down dough and then turn out onto a lightly floured surface. Cut into 2 equal pieces and then turn the bowl upside down over the dough and let rest for 15 minutes. Shape each dough piece into a ball and place balls of dough on a greased cookie sheet. Flatten tops slightly. Cover with a towel and let rise again until the dough has doubled, about 1 hour.

Preheat oven to 350°. Brush loaves with 2 T. melted butter and bake 35 minutes or until done. Set them on wire racks as soon as you remove them from the oven so the bottoms don't get soggy.

Sour Cream Dill Bread

2¼ tsp. (1 package) active dry yeast
¼ cup warm water
½ tsp. salt
1 T. butter, melted
1 cup sour cream
1 small onion, minced
2 tsp. dill weed
2 T. sugar
½ tsp. baking soda
1 egg
3 cups all-purpose flour
1 T. melted butter
coarse salt (optional)

In a large bowl, dissolve yeast in warm water. Set aside for 5 minutes. Stir in salt, butter, sour cream, onion, dill weed, sugar, baking soda, and egg. Add half of the flour and beat well. Add enough remaining flour to make a stiff dough.

Turn out onto a floured surface and knead 5 to 10 minutes. Return the dough to the bowl, cover, and let rise until double, about 1 hour.

Divide dough equally in half and shape into 2 loaves. Place in greased bread pans or on a greased baking sheet that has been dusted with cornmeal. Cover and let rise again 30 to 40 minutes.

Bake at 350° for 40 minutes. Immediately upon removing from the oven, brush the tops of loaves with melted butter, and if desired sprinkle with coarse salt.

Sunflower Flax Seed Bread

1 cup warm water
2¼ tsp. (1 package) active dry yeast
2 tsp. plus ⅓ cup sugar
⅓ cup vegetable oil
1 tsp. salt
3¼ cups all-purpose flour
½ cup unsalted sunflower seeds plus 1 T. for top
¼ cup flax seeds
1 beaten egg white

In a large bowl or stand mixer, combine the warm water, yeast, and 2 tsp. sugar. Set aside until bubbly, about 10 minutes.

Add ⅓ cup sugar, oil, salt, seeds, and approximately half the flour and mix until well combined. Continue adding flour a bit at a time until the dough pulls away from the side of the bowl.

Turn out dough onto a clean, floured surface and knead for about 8 to 10 minutes, adding additional flour, if necessary, to keep the dough from sticking.

Place the dough in a large greased bowl and turn the dough so all sides are coated. Cover with a towel and let rise until double, about 2 hours.

Punch down the dough and knead again for 1 minute. Loaf up and place the dough into a greased loaf pan.

Cover with a towel and let rise again until almost double, about 1 hour.

Preheat oven to 375°. Brush top of bread with the beaten egg white and sprinkle 1 tablespoon sunflower seeds on top. Bake 35 to 40 minutes or until done. Immediately turn out the bread onto a rack to cool completely.

Three Flours Bread

2 cups whole wheat flour
2 cups rye flour
2 cups all-purpose flour
2 cups buttermilk or regular milk
2 T. plus 1 tsp. brown sugar
1 T. molasses
½ tsp. salt
1 cup warm water
2 T. active dry yeast, rounded
¾ cup shortening or lard, melted

In a large bowl, mix together the wheat, rye, and all-purpose flours. Set aside for now.

Heat the buttermilk to warm. In a large bowl, mix warm buttermilk with 2 tablespoons brown sugar, molasses, and salt.

In a small bowl, mix together the warm water and 1 tsp. brown sugar. Sprinkle the yeast into the water and let it set until it begins to bubble and rise. Next, pour this into the large bowl containing the buttermilk mixture and stir to mix.

Now, using a large wooden spoon or an electric mixer set on low speed, spoon enough of the mixed flour into the bowl of liquid to form a stiff batter. At this point, add the melted shortening and beat the dough until it is smooth. Let the dough rest for 15 minutes.

Continue adding the flour until you have a soft bread dough. If you run out of the mixed flour, you can add some all-purpose or whole wheat flour until the dough is the right consistency.

Turn out the dough onto a floured surface and knead for 8 to 10 minutes. Place the dough in a greased bowl, turning it to coat the entire surface of the dough. Cover dough with a towel and let rise until double. Punch down and then knead lightly for 2 minutes. Grease the dough, cover it, and let it rise again until double.

Shape into 3 loaves, place them in greased bread pans, and let them rise until almost double. Bake at 350° for 45 to 60 minutes or until done.

Walnut Bread

1½ cups warm water
1 T. active dry yeast
pinch of sugar
½ cup honey
¼ cup walnut or olive oil
1½ tsp. salt
6 cups all-purpose flour, approximately
¾ cup chopped walnuts, lightly toasted
cornmeal or semolina for sprinkling

In a large bowl, gently mix the yeast, sugar, and ½ cup of flour into the warm water. Let rest for 10 minutes, until the mixture is bubbly. Stir in the honey, oil, and salt. Using an electric mixer with a bread hook or a large wooden spoon, add flour 1 cup at a time, mixing as you go. When the dough starts to pull away from the sides of the bowl, turn the dough out onto a lightly floured surface. Knead the dough for about 8 to 10 minutes, adding small amounts of flour as needed to keep it from sticking to the work surface. Place the dough ball in a large greased bowl, turning the dough ball so the entire surface is coated. Cover with a towel and let rise until double, about 1½ hours.

Punch down the dough and knead in the walnuts. Divide the dough in half and form each half into a smaller ball. Place the balls of dough on cookie sheets that have been greased and lightly sprinkled with cornmeal or semolina flour. Cover the loaves with a clean towel and let rise again until almost double, about 45 minutes.

Preheat the oven to 350°. While the oven is preheating, sprinkle a tiny amount of flour on the top of the loaves, and using a serrated knife, make a slash or cross on the top of the loaves about 1 inch deep.

Bake 35 to 45 minutes or until done. Cool on a rack and wait at least 20 minutes before cutting.

Wheat Bread

2¼ tsp. (1 package) active dry yeast
2 cups lukewarm water
2 T. sugar
2 tsp. salt
3 cups all-purpose flour
½ cup hot water
⅓ cup brown sugar
2 T. shortening
1 T. oil
3 cups whole wheat flour

In a large mixing bowl, mix yeast and lukewarm water and allow to stand for 10 minutes. Add sugar, salt, and all-purpose flour. Using a wooden spoon or electric mixer, beat mixture until smooth. Set in a warm place until light and bubbly (this is called a "sponge").

Meanwhile, combine hot water with brown sugar, shortening, and oil. Heat to lukewarm. Add to sponge and mix well with a wooden spoon. Add whole wheat flour and mix. Turn out onto a floured surface and knead for about 8 minutes, adding enough flour so it doesn't stick. The dough should be smooth and elastic. Cover and let rise until double, about 1 hour. Divide into 2 greased loaf pans and let rise until dough reaches the top of the pan (don't let it rise too high or it will fall during baking).

Bake at 375° for 35 to 40 minutes or until done.

Wheat Bread—Large Batch

4 cups hot water, not boiling
1 cup powdered milk
1 cup honey
2 heaping T. active dry yeast
2 scant T. salt
1 cup oil
4 cups whole wheat flour
12 cups all-purpose flour, more or less

In a large bowl, mix together the water, milk, honey, yeast, salt, and oil. Let stand for 10 minutes.

Add the whole wheat flour and mix well. Begin adding the all-purpose flour. When the dough leaves the sides of the bowl and you can no longer mix with a spoon, turn out dough onto a floured surface and continue adding the flour as you knead. Knead for about 8 to 10 minutes.

Cover and let rise until double, about 1 hour. Divide into 4 balls, form into loaves, place each into a greased loaf pan, and let rise slightly before baking.

Bake at 350° for 30 to 40 minutes or until done.

White Bread

1 T. active dry yeast
¼ cup warm water
1 tsp. sugar
¼ cup butter
1 T. salt
2 T. light brown sugar
1 cup warm milk
¾ cup warm water
6 cups all-purpose flour

In a small bowl, stir together the yeast, ¼ cup warm water, and 1 teaspoon sugar. Let set until the yeast is dissolved and begins to bubble and rise.

In a large bowl, stir together the butter, salt, brown sugar, milk, and ¾ cup warm water. Add the yeast mixture and stir again. Add 2 cups flour and beat with an electric mixer on low speed for 1 minute. Increase speed to medium and beat for another 2 minutes. (If beating by hand, beat for 300 strokes.) Stir in enough additional flour by hand to make a soft dough that pulls away from the sides of the bowl.

Turn the dough out onto a floured surface and knead for 8 to 10 minutes.

Grease a bowl well with shortening. Place the dough ball in the bowl, turning the dough to grease all surfaces. Cover with a towel and let rise until double. Punch down and knead again for 8 to 10 minutes. Cover dough with a towel and let rest for 20 minutes.

Shape into 2 loaves and place in 2 greased loaf pans. Cover with a towel and let rise until the dough reaches slightly above the top of the pans.

Bake at 350° for 40 minutes or until done.

Whole Wheat Milk Bread

2 cups milk
⅓ cup plus 2 T. shortening
⅓ cup sugar
1 T. salt
3 T. active dry yeast
1 cup warm water
2 cups whole wheat flour
1 cup cold water
all-purpose flour

Scald the milk by bringing it to just under a boil. Remove from heat and add the shortening, sugar, and salt and stir until dissolved.

In a small bowl, mix the yeast and warm water and allow to set until the yeast is dissolved and begins to bubble and rise.

Pour the scalded milk into a large bowl, add the whole wheat flour, and beat with a wooden spoon or with an electric mixer on low speed until thoroughly mixed and smooth. Add the yeast mixture and the cold water and mix well again. Add enough all-purpose flour to make a soft dough that pulls away from the edges of the bowl.

Turn out the dough onto a floured surface and knead 8 to 10 minutes. Place the dough in a large greased bowl, turning the dough to grease the surfaces. Cover with a towel and let rise until double in size.

Punch down the dough and gently knead for several minutes. Return dough to the greased bowl, turning it to grease the surfaces, cover with a towel, and let the dough rise a second time until double.

Shape dough into 3 loaves and spank them hard before placing them in 3 greased loaf pans. Cover with a towel and let them rise until just above the top of the pan.

Bake at 350° for 50 to 60 minutes or until done.

100% Whole Wheat Bread

2 to 2½ cups warm water (use less when weather is
    humid, more when weather is dry)
4½ tsp. (2 packets) active dry yeast
½ cup oil
½ cup molasses or honey
½ cup nonfat dry milk powder
2½ tsp. salt
7 cups whole wheat flour

Pour ¼ cup of the warm water into a large bowl and
sprinkle the yeast on top. Allow to sit for about 10 minutes or until the mixture bubbles. Add the remaining
warm water, oil, molasses or honey, milk powder, salt,
and about half of the flour.

With a heavy wooden spoon, stir the ingredients together
and then beat for about 5 minutes, gradually adding
more flour until the dough begins to pull away from the
bowl. (You can also use an electric mixer for this part.)

Place the dough ball on a clean, floured work surface and
knead for 8 to 10 minutes, adding flour only as needed.
Do your best to use as little flour as possible—the goal
with whole wheat is to have a soft dough that isn't too dry.

Place the dough ball in a large, well-greased bowl. Roll
the dough around the bowl until all surfaces have been
greased. Cover the bowl with a clean towel and let rise
until double, about 1½ to 2 hours.

Punch down the dough, knead again for a minute or two,
and place it back in the greased bowl, making sure that all
surfaces are once again greased. Cover with a towel and
let rise again until nearly double, about 1 to 1½ hours.

Punch down dough and shape into 2 loaves. Place the
loaves in greased loaf pans and cover again with the towel.
Let rise until about 1 inch above the top of the pans.

Preheat oven to 350°. Bake 35 to 40 minutes. If the top crust looks like it's getting too dark, cover it with an aluminum foil tent for the last 15 minutes.

When baking is complete, turn out the loaves onto a cooling rack and allow to cool completely before slicing. For a softer crust, rub some butter over the top crust as soon as the loaves are out of the oven.

BAGELS, BUNS, PIZZA CRUSTS, AND MORE

Godliness with contentment is great gain...
And having food and raiment let us be therewith content.

1 Timothy 6:6,8

The recipes in this chapter are just plain fun to make—and eat! Even if you are a seasoned bread baker, you may not have tried baking your own bagels or English muffins. Some of these recipes use yeast and need a bit of time to complete, but some of them—such as crackers—are ready in no time at all, and the results are delicious. Play around with the ingredients. Use what you have available. Who knows? Soon you may have "invented" a delicious recipe you can call your very own!

BAGELS

Basic Bagels

4½ cups all-purpose flour, approximately
4½ tsp. (2 packages) active dry yeast
1½ cups warm water
3 T. sugar
1 T. salt

In a large mixing bowl, combine 1½ cups flour and yeast.

In a separate bowl, combine the warm water, sugar, and salt and then add this to the flour mixture. Beat at low speed for about 30 seconds, scraping sides of bowl constantly. Beat for 3 minutes on high speed.

Stir in as much of the remaining flour as you can and then turn out onto a lightly floured surface. Knead while continuing to add enough flour to make a moderately stiff dough. Continue kneading until smooth and elastic. Cover and allow to rest for 15 minutes.

Cut dough into 12 portions and shape each into a smooth ball. Punch a hole in the middle of each with a floured finger. Pull gently to enlarge the hole to about 2 inches across.

Place the bagels on a greased baking sheet, cover, and allow to rise for 20 minutes. Bring a large kettle of water to a gentle boil, place the bagels in the boiling water for about 10 to 15 seconds, and then remove and allow to drain for a moment before placing them on a greased baking sheet.

Bake 8 to 10 minutes at 350°, and then broil them for about 90 seconds on each side to brown.

Blueberry Bagels

1 batch of Basic Bagels, unbaked
1 to 2 T. sugar
⅛ tsp. ground cinnamon
⅛ tsp. lemon zest (optional)
½ to ¾ cup dried blueberries

Before kneading the Basic Bagels, increase sugar by 1 to 2 tablespoons according to your taste preference and add the cinnamon and lemon zest. Add the blueberries last and knead them evenly through the dough.

Note: You can actually use fresh blueberries if you desire, but be forewarned that they will color the entire bagel blue. Dried blueberries may produce a streak of color through the dough but won't entirely color it.

Cheese and Jalapeño Bagels

1½ cups warm water
4 tsp. (about 2 packages) active dry yeast
1½ tsp. salt
2 T. sugar, divided
4 cups all-purpose flour, approximately
⅓ cup fresh jalapeños, seeded and minced
¾ cup Cheddar cheese, divided
1 egg beaten with 1 T. water (optional)

Combine warm water, yeast, salt, and 1 tablespoon of sugar. Let set for about 10 minutes or until mixture begins to froth.

Add flour and mix with a heavy wooden spoon or stand mixer. When the dough comes together and leaves the sides of the bowl, turn out the dough ball onto a floured surface and knead for 10 minutes, adding more flour if necessary. The dough needs to be firm but still smooth and elastic. Now add the jalapeños and half of the Cheddar cheese and knead them into the dough for an additional 2 minutes. Cover and let rise for 1 hour.

Line a baking sheet with cooking parchment paper and spray the parchment lightly with oil. (If you don't have parchment paper, spray a baking sheet with oil and then sprinkle on a small amount of cornmeal or semolina flour, i.e. Cream of Wheat). Even if you use oiled parchment paper, you can still sprinkle on a bit of cornmeal if desired.

Turn the dough out onto a lightly floured surface (use as little flour as possible) and divide the dough into at least 8 equal pieces, depending on the size of bagel you desire. Roll each dough piece into a ball. Using your fingers, poke a hole through the center of each ball and stretch into a doughnut shape. Place the bagels on the parchment-lined baking sheet, cover, and let them rise for 30 minutes.

Preheat the oven to 400° and bring 1 gallon of water to a gentle boil in a large, wide pot.

Using a slotted spoon, carefully drop bagels into the pot of boiling water, a few at a time because you don't want to crowd them. Boil for 1 minute and then flip the bagels and boil them for an additional minute. Remove the bagels with the slotted spoon and place them back on the parchment-lined baking sheet.

If you are using the beaten egg, now is the time to brush the tops of the bagels with the egg wash. Sprinkle the remaining Cheddar cheese on the tops. Work quickly so the cheese adheres well before the tops dry out.

Bake 20 to 22 minutes or until the bagels are done and have turned golden brown. Remove the bagels from the oven and place on racks to cool.

Cinnamon Raisin Bagels

4½ tsp. (2 packages) yeast
1½ cups warm water
2 T. sugar
1 tsp. salt
4 cups all-purpose flour
1 slightly heaping T. cinnamon
1½ cups raisins
1 gallon water
1 T. honey

In a large bowl, mix together the yeast, warm water, sugar, and salt. Let set for about 10 minutes or until frothy. Beat in 2 cups of the flour and the cinnamon using an electric mixer or a large wooden spoon. Add in the raisins and mix again. Gradually add the remaining 2 cups flour and stir with a wooden spoon. When the dough leaves the sides of the bowl, turn it out onto a floured surface and knead for about 5 minutes. Divide the dough into 12 balls, poke a hole in the middle of each ball with your finger, and place each ball on a greased pan. Cover and allow to rise for 30 minutes.

Preheat oven to 350°. Grease a very large cookie sheet (you might need to use an additional sheet) and set aside.

Bring the gallon of water and honey to a rolling boil. Gently lift bagels and place them, about 3 at a time so they aren't crowded, into the boiling honey water. Once all 3 are in the boiling water, turn them with a slotted spoon. Boil them about 30 seconds total. Drain on absorbent paper or cloth towels and then place the bagels on the greased cookie sheet. Bake 30 minutes. Remove from oven and cool on a wire rack.

BAGELS, BUNS, PIZZA CRUSTS...

Everything Bagels

4 tsp. poppy seeds
4 tsp. sesame seeds
4 tsp. dried minced garlic
4 tsp. dried minced onion
2 tsp. coarse salt
1 batch of Basic Bagels, unbaked

Combine all topping ingredients and mix together thoroughly. Sprinkle over the top of bagels before baking as directed in the Basic Bagel recipe.

CRACKERS

Graham Crackers

2 cups whole wheat flour
2 tsp. baking powder
¼ tsp. salt
4 T. brown sugar
½ cup butter
2 T. honey
2 T. milk
dash of vanilla
cinnamon sugar

Mix together all ingredients except cinnamon sugar. Turn out onto a cookie sheet and roll out thinly and evenly. Sprinkle surface with cinnamon sugar and lightly press sugar mixture into surface of dough. Deeply score dough in squares (a pizza cutter works well).

Bake at 375° for 8 minutes. Allow to cool slightly before cutting through crackers.

Olive Oil and Sesame Seed Crackers

2 cups all-purpose flour (or a combination of all-
    purpose and whole wheat flour if desired)
¾ tsp. salt
¼ cup olive oil
½ cup water, approximately
coarse salt
¼ cup sesame seeds

In a mixing bowl, mix together the flour and salt. Add the olive oil and water and gently mix, adding more water if needed to bring the dough together into a ball.

Roll the dough out on a floured surface to ⅛-inch thick. Score dough into 2-inch squares (a pizza cutter works well). Prick each square with a fork. Sprinkle dough with coarse salt and sesame seeds.

Bake in a preheated 350° oven 15 to 20 minutes or until crackers are crisp and a light golden color.

Soda Crackers

Yeast mixture:
¼ cup warm water
1 T. yeast

In a small bowl mix together the yeast and warm water; set aside.

Baking soda mixture:
1 tsp. baking soda
2 T. warm water

In another small bowl mix together the baking soda and warm water; set aside.

1¾ cups water
baking soda mixture
yeast mixture
⅔ cup oil or melted shortening or lard
4 cups flour, approximately
1 T. salt

In a large bowl, mix together the water, baking soda mixture, yeast mixture, and oil or melted shortening until well blended. Add enough flour so the dough pulls away from the sides of the bowl. Turn out the dough and knead for 10 minutes, adding flour as needed. (You'll use about 4 cups of flour total.)

Divide dough into several small portions so it's easier to work. Roll dough ⅛-inch thick. Cut into squares. Prick with fork.

Bake at 350° for until lightly browned, about 10 minutes.

Store in a can or jar with a tight fitting lid.

Whole Wheat Crackers

2 cups whole wheat flour
1 tsp. salt
½ cup sesame seeds
¼ cup wheat germ
¼ cup oil
¼ cup Parmesan cheese
½ cup water (slightly more if needed)

Mix together all ingredients. Add enough water to hold dough together. Roll out on a floured surface (thinner dough makes crisper crackers) and cut into desired shapes.

Bake on an ungreased cookie sheet at 350° for 8 to 10 minutes.

ENGLISH MUFFINS

Cinnamon Raisin English Muffins

⅓ cup warm water
1 T. sugar
2¼ tsp. (1 package) active dry yeast
1 cup slightly warm milk (nonfat milk works well in
    this recipe)
¾ tsp. salt
1 tsp. ground cinnamon
2 cups all-purpose flour
⅓ cup raisins

In a large bowl, mix together the water, sugar, and yeast. Let stand for 10 minutes or until bubbly.

To the yeast mixture, add all remaining ingredients except the raisins. Using a large wooden spoon, stir the mixture until it comes together and is smooth. Add raisins and mix thoroughly. Cover the bowl with a clean towel and let it rest for 1 hour.

Heat a griddle or frying pan on a medium-low setting and lightly grease the bottom of the griddle or pan. Drop ¼ cup of dough at a time onto the pan and cook the muffins until the bottom is golden brown. Flip the muffins over, flatten slightly, and cook the second side until golden brown also. Your goal is to cook the English muffins completely, so keep the temperature low enough so that it takes more than 5 minutes to brown each side.

Remove the English muffins to a rack to cool thoroughly before serving. Split the English muffins using a fork instead of a knife.

Oven Baked Wheat English Muffins

2¼ tsp. (1 package) active dry yeast
3 T. sugar, divided
¼ cup warm water
1 cup warm milk
3 T. butter
¾ tsp. salt
1 egg, beaten
1½ cups whole wheat flour
2½ cups all-purpose flour

In a large bowl, dissolve the yeast and 1 tablespoon sugar in the warm water. Let stand for about 5 minutes or until the mixture is bubbly. Add the milk, butter, salt, egg, remaining sugar, and whole wheat flour, and using a large wooden spoon or an electric mixer set on low speed, beat until smooth. Stir in enough all-purpose flour to form a soft dough.

Turn out the dough onto a clean, floured work surface and knead the dough about 6 to 8 minutes or until the dough is satiny smooth and elastic. Place the dough ball in a large greased bowl and turn the dough until all surfaces are greased. Cover the bowl with a clean towel and let rise until double, about 1½ hours.

Punch down the dough and then turn it out onto a clean, lightly floured surface. Roll out to ½-inch thick and then allow to rest for 5 minutes. Cut the dough into 4-inch circles and place them 2 inches apart on greased baking sheets.

Preheat oven to 375°. Bake about 8 minutes or until the bottoms are brown. Turn the English muffins over and continue baking for another 7 minutes or until the second side is brown. Remove the baked English muffins to wire racks to cool. When ready to serve, split them in half if desired using a fork.

Plain English Muffins

1¾ cups warm milk (heat to about 115°)
2¼ tsp. (1 package) active dry yeast
3 T. butter, softened
1¼ tsp. salt
2 T. sugar
1 egg
4½ cups all-purpose flour
cornmeal for sprinkling

In a large bowl, mix together the warm milk and yeast. Let this sit for 10 minutes or until the yeast is bubbly.

Add the butter, salt, sugar, egg, and flour and mix by hand or with an electric mixer for 5 minutes—the dough will be very soft and sticky.

Scrape the dough out into another large bowl that has been greased (you can use shortening, oil, or butter) and cover with a clean towel. Let the dough rise for 2 hours.

Grease your hands and pinch off small pieces of dough. Form each piece into a ball and place them on a large baking sheet that has been generously sprinkled with cornmeal or covered with greased parchment paper. Flatten the balls by gently pressing down on the tops. Let them rest for 20 minutes.

Preheat a griddle or heavy pan (cast iron works well) on a medium-low setting. Carefully transfer the English muffins to the preheated griddle, making sure not to crowd them in the pan, and cook until the bottoms are a deep golden brown. Flip the English muffins and continue to cook them until that side is deep golden brown also.

Transfer the cooked English muffins to a rack to cool completely before serving. Use a fork to split them open.

PRETZELS

Soft Pretzels

1 T. sugar
2 tsp. salt
1½ cups warm water
2¼ tsp. (1 package) active dry yeast
4½ cups all-purpose flour
4 T. butter, melted
3 qts. water
⅔ cup baking soda
1 egg yolk plus 1 tablespoon water, whisked together
    (for egg wash)
coarse salt

Combine the sugar, salt, and water in a mixing bowl and sprinkle the yeast on top. Let set for about 5 minutes or until the mixture begins to foam.

Add the flour and butter, and using an electric mixer or a large wooden spoon, mix well. Continue mixing until the dough pulls away from the side of the bowl. Dump dough out onto a clean, floured surface and knead about 5 to 7 minutes.

Place dough ball into a large oiled bowl, turning dough ball until all surfaces are greased. Cover with a clean towel and let rise until double, about 1 hour.

Preheat oven to 450°. Line 2 baking sheets with parchment paper that has been greased, or grease the baking sheets and sprinkle with cornmeal. Set aside for now.

In a large, wide pot, add about 3 quarts water and the baking soda. Heat the water on high and stir to completely mix and dissolve the baking soda. While the soda water is heating, divide the dough into 8 or more equal portions. Roll out each piece into a long rope and then shape the pretzels. (Try making a U shape with the rope.

Holding the ends of the rope, cross them over each other and bring them down through the center of the U. Then press the ends onto the bottom of the U.) Set the pretzels on the baking sheets and continue until all the pretzels have been shaped.

Carefully place the pretzels, about 2 or 3 at a time so you don't crowd them, in the pot of boiling soda water and parboil for 30 seconds. Remove them from the boiling water using a large spatula or suitable strainer and place the pretzels back on the baking sheets. When all of the pretzels have been parboiled, brush the tops with the egg wash and sprinkle with coarse salt.

Bake the pretzels for 12 to 14 minutes until golden brown and done. Transfer to a cooling rack and let them rest for at least 5 minutes before serving.

Other toppings for your pretzels: Instead of sprinkling salt on top, try using cinnamon and sugar, grated pepper jack or Cheddar cheese, finely chopped onion, garlic, poppy seeds, or sesame seeds.

- -

Yeast-Free Soft Pretzels

2 cups all-purpose flour
3 T. butter
2 T. white sugar
2 tsp. baking powder
pinch of salt
⅓ cup whole milk or half-and-half
small amount of cornmeal
1 egg, beaten
coarse salt

Mix together the flour and butter until crumbs form. Add sugar, baking powder, and salt and mix together. Add milk slowly, mixing as you pour, until all the ingredients are wet. You may not need all of the milk, so go slowly. Conversely, you may need a bit more milk. When thoroughly mixed, you want the dough to come away from the bowl and look like a ball—not too sticky, but also not too dry. There is no need to let the dough rest so you can begin forming pretzels immediately.

Prepare your baking sheets by greasing them and then lightly sprinkling with cornmeal.

Divide the dough into smaller balls (about 10 to 12 is a good number, but you can make them larger or smaller depending on preference). Using the palms of your hands, roll out each ball into a long snake. Twist them into shape and place them on the prepared baking sheets. Once you have made all your pretzels, brush them with the beaten egg and sprinkle with coarse salt.

Bake in preheated 350° oven 10 minutes (you may need to bake them a bit longer depending on the size of your pretzels) or until golden.

ROLLS, BUNS, AND PIZZA CRUSTS

Dinner Rolls

2 T. sugar
2 T. shortening, melted and cooled
1½ tsp. salt
2¼ tsp. (1 package) active dry yeast
1 cup lukewarm water
3¼ cups all-purpose flour

Add the sugar, shortening, salt, and yeast to the lukewarm water and let sit until bubbly, about 10 minutes. Add 1 cup of the flour and beat until smooth. Then by hand, mix in the remaining flour. Place the dough on a floured board and let it rest for about 5 minutes.

Knead the dough, adding small amounts of flour as needed, until smooth and elastic. Round into a ball and place the dough into a greased bowl, turning to grease all surfaces. Cover it and allow the dough to rise for 1 hour.

Pat out dough into a rectangle and roll up jelly-roll style. (Spread some softened butter on the dough before rolling it up if you want butter rolls.) Cut the log into 1-inch slices and place the rolls, cut side up, on a greased baking sheet.

Bake at 450° for 12 to 15 minutes.

Hamburger or Hot Dog Buns

2 T. active dry yeast
1 cup plus 2 T. warm water
⅓ cup vegetable oil
¼ cup sugar
1 egg
1 tsp. salt
3 to 3½ cups all-purpose flour

In a large bowl, dissolve the yeast in the warm water. Add oil and sugar, mix again, and let set until the yeast begins to bubble and rise, about 10 minutes. Add the egg, salt, and enough flour to form a soft dough.

Turn out onto a floured surface and knead until smooth, about 5 minutes. Do not let rise.

Divide the dough into 12 pieces and shape each into a ball for a hamburger bun or a log for a hot dog bun. Place them 3 inches apart on greased cookie sheets.

Cover and let rest for 15 minutes. Bake at 425° for 8 to 12 minutes or until golden brown and done. Cool on wire racks and then slice them in half lengthwise to serve.

Hoagie Sandwich Rolls

2¼ tsp. (1 package) active dry yeast
3 cups warm water, divided
2 T. sugar, divided
¼ cup oil
1 T. salt
8 to 8 ½ cups all-purpose flour

In a large bowl, dissolve the yeast and 1 tablespoon sugar in ½ cup warm water. Let stand about 5 minutes or until bubbly.

Add the remaining water and sugar and mix in oil, salt, and 4 cups flour. Using a stand mixer or a large wooden spoon, beat until flour mixture is smooth. Stir in enough flour to form a soft dough.

Turn out onto a floured surface and knead for 6 to 8 minutes or until smooth and elastic. Place the ball of kneaded dough into a large greased bowl, turning the dough so all surfaces are greased. Cover and let rise until double, about 1 hour.

Punch down dough and turn out onto a lightly floured surface. Divide dough into 18 equal pieces. Shape each piece of dough into an oval and place them 2 inches apart on greased baking sheets. With a very sharp knife or kitchen scissors, slash the top of each piece ¼ inch deep. Cover with a towel and let rise for 20 minutes.

Bake in a preheated 400° oven 13 to 18 minutes or until light golden brown. Cool on wire racks before cutting open.

Jiffy Pizza Crust

2 cups all-purpose flour
1 T. baking powder
1 tsp. salt
⅔ cup milk
⅓ cup oil

Mix together the flour, baking powder, and salt. Add the milk and oil and mix to make a soft dough.

Pat out on a lightly greased pizza pan or baking sheet. Top with your favorite pizza sauce and toppings and bake in a preheated 425° oven 25 to 30 minutes.

Mashed Potato Rolls

2¼ tsp. (1 package) active dry yeast
¼ cup warm water
1¾ cups warm milk
¼ cup butter, softened (room temperature)
¼ cup oil
6 T. sugar
1 egg
½ cup mashed potatoes (see note at end of recipe)
1½ tsp. salt
1 tsp. baking powder
½ tsp. baking soda
6 cups all-purpose flour
melted butter (optional)

In a large bowl, dissolve yeast in warm water. Add milk, butter, oil, sugar, egg, and mashed potatoes and mix well. Stir in salt, baking powder, baking soda, and half the flour. Mix either by hand or using a stand mixer, adding flour until a soft dough is formed.

Turn out onto a floured surface and knead 6 to 8 minutes or until the dough is smooth and elastic.

Place the dough in a large greased bowl and turn so the entire surface of the dough is greased. Cover with a clean towel and let rise until double, about 1½ hours.

Punch down dough. Turn out onto a lightly floured surface and shape bits of dough into approximately 32 round balls. Place balls 2 inches apart on greased baking sheets. Cover and let rise until double, about 30 to 45 minutes.

Bake in a preheated 375° oven 15 to 18 minutes or until done and golden. Remove from the oven and if desired immediately brush or dip tops of rolls in melted butter. Set on racks to cool.

Note: If you don't have any leftover mashed potatoes and you're in a hurry, you can use dehydrated mashed potatoes. Just mix according to the package directions and use in place of fresh mashed potatoes.

Overnight Butterhorns

2¼ tsp. (1 package) active dry yeast
1 cup warm water, divided
½ cup sugar, divided
3 eggs, beaten
½ cup melted butter plus about ½ cup more for dipping
1 tsp. salt
4½ to 5 cups all-purpose flour

The night before, mix together the yeast, ¼ cup warm water, and 1 tsp. sugar in a large bowl. Let stand for 10 minutes or until bubbly. Add the rest of the water and sugar and mix. Add the beaten eggs, ½ cup melted butter, salt, and 2 cups of the flour. Mix well, continuing to add flour until the dough pulls away from the side of the bowl and forms a soft ball.

Turn dough out onto a floured surface and knead for 4 to 5 minutes. Place the dough in a large greased bowl, turning the dough so all surfaces are greased. Cover and place in the refrigerator overnight.

The next day, roll out the dough in a circle shape and cut into pie shaped wedges. Roll each piece up and dip them into melted butter before placing them on a baking sheet about 3 inches apart. Cover loosely with plastic wrap and let them rise for 3 hours.

Bake in a preheated 325° oven about 20 minutes or until golden brown.

Overnight No-Knead Butter Rolls

4½ tsp. (2 packages) yeast
1¼ cups warm water, divided
3 eggs
5 cups all-purpose flour
½ cup sugar
¾ cup melted butter, divided
2 tsp. salt
at least ½ cup softened butter for spreading

In a small bowl, sprinkle the yeast over ¼ cup of the warm water and let set until it begins to froth and bubble, about 10 minutes.

In a large mixing bowl, beat the eggs and then blend the eggs into the dissolved yeast mixture. Add 2½ cups of the flour, alternating with the remaining warm water. Add the sugar, ½ cup of the melted butter, and the salt and mix until smooth. Beat in the remaining flour to make a soft dough. Cover with a towel and let rise until double, about 1½ to 2 hours. Punch down dough, cover with plastic wrap, and refrigerate overnight.

The next day, punch down the dough and divide in half. On a floured surface, roll out each half into an 8 x 15-inch rectangle. Spread with lots of softened butter. Starting with a long edge, roll up dough jelly-roll style. With a very sharp knife, cut into 1-inch-thick slices. Place slices in greased muffin tin cups, cut side up. Cover and let rise until double, about 1 hour.

Bake in a preheated 400° oven 8 to 10 minutes or until rolls are golden brown. Immediately upon removing from the oven, brush tops with the remaining melted butter. Remove from muffin tins and cool on a wire rack.

Pizza Crust

1 cup warm water
4½ tsp. (2 packages) active dry yeast
1 tsp. sugar
1 tsp. basil, optional
¼ tsp. garlic powder, optional
½ tsp. salt
2½ cups all-purpose flour, approximately

Combine water, yeast, and sugar. Let sit 5 minutes. Add rest of ingredients and mix into dough. Turn the dough onto a floured surface and knead until smooth, 5 to 7 minutes. Let rest for 20 minutes.

Grease a pizza pan or cookie sheet and press out dough to fit the pan.

Bake 7 minutes in a preheated 400° oven. Take out and top with pizza sauce or a thin layer of tomato paste and your favorite toppings. Return the pizza to the oven to bake an additional 8 to 12 minutes or until done.

Quick and Easy Pizza Crust

2¼ tsp. (1 package) instant yeast ("Rapid Rise")
1 cup warm water, divided
1 T. oil
1 tsp. sugar
1 tsp. salt
2½ cups all-purpose flour
cornmeal for dusting pizza pan

In a large bowl, dissolve yeast in ¼ cup warm water. When thoroughly dissolved, add the remaining ¾ cup warm water, oil, sugar, salt, and flour. Using a large wooden spoon, mix until the dough pulls away from the side of the bowl and becomes a ball. Let rest for 10 minutes.

Preheat the oven to 425°. Grease a pizza pan or baking sheet and lightly dust with cornmeal.

Turn out the dough onto a lightly floured surface and knead for 2 minutes. Shape the dough to fit the size of the pizza pan and transfer the dough.

Top with pizza sauce or a thin layer of tomato paste and your favorite toppings and bake 20 minutes or until done.

Quick Cloverleaf Rolls

2¼ tsp. (1 package) active dry yeast
1¼ cups warm water
¼ cup sugar
½ tsp. salt
2 eggs
2 T. oil
4½ to 5 cups all-purpose flour
butter (optional)

In a large mixing bowl, dissolve yeast and a pinch of sugar in the warm water. Let set for 10 minutes. Add the sugar and salt and mix together. Beat in eggs one at a time using an electric mixer or a large wooden spoon with vigorous strokes. Add oil and beat again to blend.

Gradually beat in 2 to 3 cups flour and keep beating the mixture for 3 minutes. Continue to add flour until the dough begins to form a soft ball and leaves the sides of the bowl.

Turn out ball of dough onto a floured surface and with buttered hands, gently knead for 3 minutes, adding small bits of flour if necessary. This dough is very soft and sticky, but persevere. Keeping your hands buttered will help.

Grease a muffin tin. Keeping your hands well-buttered, break off small pieces of dough and roll into balls about the size of large marbles. Place 3 balls of dough in each muffin tin cup and gently press down. Cover and let rise in a warm place for 30 to 40 minutes.

Bake in a preheated 400° oven 15 to 17 minutes or until very lightly browned. Remove from oven and immediately brush tops with butter. Remove the rolls from the muffin tin and place on a rack to cool.

Rachael's Cracked Wheat Potato Rolls

¾ cup cracked wheat
1 cup butter
3 cups boiling water
2 T. yeast
⅔ cup instant potato flakes
½ cup nonfat dry milk
⅔ cup sugar
1 T. salt

2 T. wheat germ
2 eggs
7 cups all-purpose flour

In a large bowl, combine cracked wheat, butter, and boiling water. Cool to lukewarm. Add remaining ingredients but only 2 cups of the flour. Beat with a mixer for 2 minutes. Gradually add remaining flour by hand.

On a floured surface, knead 5 to 8 minutes. Place dough into a greased bowl, turning dough ball so the entire surface is greased. Cover and let rise until double, about 1 to 1½ hours. Punch down. Shape into round rolls and place on lightly greased baking sheets. Cover and let rise 30 minutes.

Bake in a preheated 350° oven 15 to 20 minutes.

Refrigerator Dinner Rolls

2¼ tsp. (1 package) active dry yeast
2 T. warm water
1 cup very hot water
1 tsp. salt
6 T. shortening
¼ cup sugar
1 egg, well beaten
3½ cups all-purpose flour

In a small bowl, combine yeast with warm water and set aside until light and bubbly, about 10 minutes.

In a large mixing bowl, combine the hot water, salt, shortening, and sugar and mix well. Cool to lukewarm. Add the yeast mixture, stir, and then add the beaten egg and half of the flour. Beat well.

With a wooden spoon (and then with your hands if necessary), stir in more of the flour, enough to make the dough easy to handle. Grease the top of the dough, cover, and store in the refrigerator for up to 1 week.

When you want to bake the dinner rolls, take out the amount of dough needed. Shape into balls and put on a greased baking pan or in muffin tins. Cover and let rise in a warm place until dough warms up and doubles in bulk, about 2 hours.

Bake at 425° for 12 to 15 minutes.

QUICK BREADS

Give us this day our daily bread.

Matthew 6:11

Quick breads can be savory or sweet. They make a great complement to a meal and a comforting dessert or snack. As the name of this chapter implies, they take much less time to mix and bake than yeast-raised breads. Quick breads generally freeze well, so make up and bake a batch or two and freeze them to have something delicious to serve your guests at a moment's notice when they unexpectedly drop by.

Apple Pecan Bread

½ cup butter
1 cup sugar
2 eggs
2 T. milk
1 tsp. vanilla
2 cups all-purpose flour
1 cup peeled, chopped apples
½ cup chopped pecans

Preheat oven to 350°. Grease a 9 x 5-inch loaf pan and set aside.

In a large mixing bowl, cream together butter and sugar until light and fluffy. Beat in the eggs, milk, and vanilla. Add flour and stir just until blended. Fold in apples and pecans. Pour into a prepared loaf pan and bake 1 hour. Remove bread from pan and cool on a rack. Once cool, wrap the bread with plastic wrap and let stand overnight before slicing.

Applesauce Nut Bread

1½ cups all-purpose flour
1 tsp. baking powder
1 tsp. baking soda
1 tsp. salt
1 tsp. cinnamon
½ tsp. nutmeg
1 cup rolled oats
½ cup chopped walnuts
½ cup raisins
⅓ cup shortening
½ cup brown sugar
2 eggs
1 cup unsweetened applesauce
½ cup milk

In a large mixing bowl, sift together the flour, baking powder, baking soda, salt, cinnamon, and nutmeg. Stir in the rolled oats, walnuts, and raisins.

In another bowl, cream together the shortening and brown sugar. Add the eggs and beat until light and fluffy. Blend in applesauce and milk.

Add creamed mixture to the dry ingredients and beat for 30 seconds. Although the batter will be lumpy, don't overbeat it. Pour batter into a large, greased loaf pan and bake at 350° for 50 to 60 minutes.

Banana Nut Bread

⅔ cup sugar
⅓ cup shortening
2 eggs
3 T. sour milk or buttermilk
1 cup mashed bananas (slightly overripe bananas work
    best)
2 cups all-purpose flour
1 tsp. baking powder
½ tsp. baking soda
½ tsp. salt
½ cup chopped walnuts

Mix together sugar, shortening, and eggs. (An electric mixer works best.) Stir in sour milk and mashed bananas.

Sift together the flour, baking powder, baking soda, and salt and blend into the banana mixture. Then add the walnuts and stir to blend.

Pour batter into a well-greased loaf pan. Let stand for 20 minutes before baking. Bake at 350° for 50 to 60 minutes.

QUICK BREADS

Carrot Bread

½ cup oil
1 cup sugar
2 eggs, beaten
1 cup shredded carrots
1½ cups all-purpose flour
1 tsp. baking soda
1 tsp. baking powder
¼ tsp. salt
1 tsp. cinnamon
½ cup milk
½ cup chopped walnuts (optional)

Mix together the oil and sugar. Add beaten eggs and mix well. Stir in the shredded carrots.

Sift together the flour, baking soda, baking powder, salt, and cinnamon. Add sugar mixture alternately with the milk, blending after each addition. If desired, fold in walnuts.

Pour batter into a greased loaf pan and bake at 350° for 55 minutes or until done.

Carrot Pineapple Bread

3 eggs
2 cups sugar
¾ cup vegetable oil
3 cups all-purpose flour
¾ tsp. cinnamon
¾ tsp. nutmeg
1 tsp. baking soda
½ tsp. salt
1 13½-oz. can crushed pineapple, undrained
½ cup chopped nuts
3 tsp. vanilla

Cream together the eggs, sugar, and oil. Stir together the flour, cinnamon, nutmeg, baking soda, and salt and then stir into the creamed mixture. Fold in the pineapple, nuts, and vanilla and blend thoroughly.

Pour batter into 2 greased loaf pans and bake in a preheated 350° oven 50 to 55 minutes or until done.

Chocolate Zucchini Bread

3 eggs, beaten
1 cup oil
1¾ cups sugar
1 T. vanilla
2 cups zucchini, grated
3 cups all-purpose flour
1 tsp. salt
1 tsp. baking soda
1 tsp. baking powder
½ cup unsweetened cocoa powder
½ cup chopped walnuts or pecans (optional)

In a large bowl, mix together the eggs, oil, sugar, and vanilla. Add the zucchini and stir.

In a separate bowl, mix together the flour, salt, baking soda, baking powder, and cocoa powder. Add dry ingredients to the zucchini mixture and blend well. If desired, add nuts and stir again.

Grease and flour 2 loaf pans and pour in batter. Bake at 350° for 45 minutes. Cool in pans for 10 to 15 minutes before removing zucchini bread to wire rack to finish cooling.

Communion Bread (Unleavened)

1½ cups all-purpose flour
2 T. sugar
½ tsp. salt
½ cup butter
½ cup milk

In a large bowl, combine the flour, sugar, and salt. Using a pastry blender or 2 knives, cut in the butter until it resembles coarse crumbs. Add the milk and mix until a stiff dough forms.

Turn out onto a floured surface and roll out very thin and uniform, about 13 x 17 inches. With a pizza cutter, even up the edges. Transfer the dough to a greased cookie sheet and use the pizza cutter to cut into 1-inch-wide strips. Prick pieces at 1-inch intervals with a fork.

Bake on lower rack in a preheated 425° oven 6 to 7 minutes. The outside strips may brown more quickly than the inside ones, so remove the outside strips and continue to bake the inner strips for a few minutes longer—but watch them carefully so they don't get too dark. Break into 1-inch pieces to serve for communion or larger pieces for a meal.

Corn Bread

1 cup all-purpose flour
1 cup cornmeal
½ cup instant dry milk
2 T. sugar
4 tsp. baking powder
½ tsp. salt
1 egg
1 cup water
¼ cup oil

Grease a 9 x 9 x 2-inch pan and set aside.

In a mixing bowl, combine flour, cornmeal, instant milk, sugar, baking powder, and salt and stir to mix well.

In a medium-sized bowl, beat egg and then add water and oil, beating until well blended. Stir into the cornmeal mixture. Beat by hand just until well blended and smooth. Pour batter into prepared pan.

Bake at 425° for 20 minutes or until done and a light golden color.

Corn Bread with Cheese and Bacon

1 cup all-purpose flour
1 cup cornmeal
½ cup instant dry milk
2 T. sugar
4 tsp. baking powder
½ tsp. salt
½ cup shredded Cheddar cheese
½ cup cooked, crumbled bacon
1 egg
1 cup water
¼ cup oil

Grease a 9 x 9 x 2-inch pan and set aside.

In a mixing bowl, combine flour, cornmeal, instant milk, sugar, baking powder, and salt and stir to mix well. Add the cheese and bacon and stir well again.

In a medium-sized bowl, beat egg and then add water and oil, beating until well blended. Stir into the cornmeal mixture. Beat by hand just until well blended and smooth. Pour batter into prepared pan. Bake at 425° for 20 to 25 minutes or until done and a light golden color.

Dutch Apple Bread

½ cup butter, room temperature
1 cup sugar
2 eggs
1 tsp. vanilla
2 cups all-purpose flour
1 T. baking soda
½ tsp. salt
⅓ cup sour milk
1 cup chopped apples
⅓ cup chopped walnuts

In a large bowl, cream together the butter and sugar. Add the eggs and vanilla and beat well.

Mix together the flour, baking soda, and salt. Add dry ingredients alternately with the milk, blending well. Fold in the chopped apples and walnuts.

Place batter into a greased 9 x 5-inch loaf pan and bake at 350° for 55 minutes or until done.

Garlic Cheese Breadsticks

½ cup butter, melted
2½ cups all-purpose flour
4 tsp. baking powder
1⅓ cups milk
2 tsp. garlic powder
Parmesan cheese to taste
dried parsley (optional)

Pour melted butter into a 9 x 13-inch baking pan. In a mixing bowl, mix together the flour, baking powder, and milk and stir until a soft dough forms. Knead about 3 minutes, adding extra flour if the dough is too sticky.

Roll out dough to form 8-inch squares. Cut each square in half and then cut into 4 x 1½-inch strips. Place the strips into the pan and turn them so both sides are buttered. Sprinkle the strips with the garlic powder, Parmesan cheese, and parsley.

Bake in a preheated 450° oven 15 to 20 minutes or until done.

Ginger Pumpkin Bread

¾ cup butter, melted
1 15-oz. can pumpkin
3 eggs
2½ cups all-purpose flour
2 tsp. baking powder
2 tsp. ground ginger
1 tsp. salt
1 cup sugar
1 cup brown sugar, packed
Sugar Glaze (recipe follows)

Whisk together the butter, pumpkin, and eggs.

Mix together the flour, baking powder, ginger, salt, sugar, and brown sugar and add to the pumpkin mixture until just combined. Do not overmix.

Divide batter between 2 greased loaf pans and bake at 375° for 50 to 55 minutes. Cool for 10 minutes and then turn out onto a rack to cool completely. If desired glaze with Sugar Glaze.

Sugar Glaze
1½ cups powdered sugar
2 to 3 T. water

Mix the powdered sugar and water together until well blended and to desired consistency. Drizzle over cooled bread.

QUICK BREADS

Green Chili Cheese Bread

1 loaf French bread (see recipe on page 27 or use a
     store-bought loaf)
1 cup mayonnaise
2 cups Monterey Jack cheese, shredded
1 can diced green chilies

Slice French bread in half lengthwise. Mix together the
mayonnaise, Monterey Jack cheese, and green chilies.
Spread half of the mixture on each half of the French
bread. Place the 2 halves on a large baking sheet and bake
in a preheated 350° oven 15 minutes or until the topping
is lightly brown and bubbly. Slice and serve immediately.

Hawaiian Bread

1 large can crushed pineapple, undrained
1 10-oz. package coconut
4 eggs
1½ cups sugar
4 cups all-purpose flour
2 tsp. salt
2 tsp. baking soda

Mix together the pineapple and coconut and add the
eggs and sugar and mix well.

In a separate bowl, sift together the flour, salt, and baking soda. Add to the pineapple mixture and mix well.
Pour the batter into 3 greased loaf pans and bake at 325°
for 1 hour.

Lemon Bread

1 lemon
2¼ cups all-purpose flour
1½ tsp. baking powder
¾ tsp. salt
1½ cups plus 2 T. sugar
¾ cup butter
3 eggs
¾ cup milk

Preheat oven to 350°.

Grate the lemon peel to make 1 tablespoon. Squeeze the lemon to make 4½ teaspoons juice.

In a large bowl and using a fork, mix together the flour, baking powder, salt, and 1½ cups sugar. With pastry blender or 2 butter knives, cut in butter until mixture resembles coarse crumbles. Stir in lemon peel.

In a small bowl, whisk the eggs slightly and then stir in the milk. Add to the flour mixture and stir just until moistened. Don't overmix. Spoon batter into a greased loaf pan and bake 1¼ hours or until done. Allow bread to cool on a wire rack in pan for 10 minutes before turning out onto the rack to finish cooling.

Meanwhile, make the lemon glaze by heating the lemon juice and 2 tablespoons of sugar in a small saucepan over medium-high heat until boiling. Turn down heat slightly and, stirring constantly, cook until slightly thickened, about 3 to 5 minutes. Remove from heat and brush the top of the cooling loaf with glaze. Serve this bread warm as a great dessert or afternoon treat or cool completely to serve later.

QUICK BREADS

Lemon Walnut Bread

⅓ cup shortening
1 cup sugar
2 eggs, well beaten
2 cups all-purpose flour, divided
1 tsp. baking powder
⅛ tsp. salt
½ cup milk
2 tsp. lemon juice
1 tsp. lemon zest
½ cup walnuts
Lemon Glaze (recipe below)

In a large bowl, cream together the shortening and sugar until light and fluffy. Add the beaten eggs and beat well again.

Sift only 1 cup of the flour together with the baking powder and salt and add to creamed mixture. Mix until smooth. Next, add the milk, lemon juice, lemon zest, and nuts and blend again. Add the remaining cup of flour and blend again.

Pour batter into a greased loaf pan and bake at 300° for 90 minutes. While hot, spread loaf with Lemon Glaze.

Lemon Glaze
½ cup powdered sugar
1 T. lemon juice

Combine ingredients and mix until smooth. Add a bit more powdered sugar or lemon juice to achieve the desired consistency. If it's too thick, try adding a few drops of milk (or just use more lemon juice).

Onion Cheese Bread

2 cups flour (all-purpose, wheat, or a combination)
1 T. sugar
3 tsp. baking powder
1 tsp. dry mustard
1 tsp. salt
¼ cup butter
½ cup shredded Cheddar cheese, plus a bit more to
    sprinkle on top
2 T. grated Parmesan cheese
1 cup milk
1 egg
½ cup finely chopped onions

In a large bowl, combine first 5 ingredients. Cut in butter until mixture resembles coarse cornmeal. Add the Cheddar and Parmesan cheeses and mix until well incorporated.

In a small bowl, mix together the milk and egg. Add all at once to the flour mixture and mix with a fork just until dry ingredients are moistened.

Turn batter into a greased loaf pan and sprinkle onions and a small amount of shredded Cheddar cheese over the top of the loaf. Bake at 350° for 55 to 60 minutes or until done.

Orange Nut Bread

grated zest of 1 orange (grate the zest only—the white
    pith has a bitter taste)
½ cup water
1 tsp. salt
½ cup sugar
milk
juice of 1 orange
1 egg, beaten
1 cup all-purpose flour
1 cup whole wheat flour
2 tsp. baking powder
¼ tsp. baking soda
¼ cup shortening
½ cup chopped nuts

Combine the orange zest, water, salt, and sugar in a
saucepan. Bring to a simmer, then turn down the heat
and cook for 10 minutes. Allow to cool.

Add milk to the juice of one orange to make a total of 1
cup. Add this mixture plus the beaten egg to the cooled
orange zest mixture.

Blend together the flours, baking powder, and baking
soda, and then cut in the shortening until the mixture
resembles coarse cornmeal.

Pour the liquid mixture into the dry ingredients and stir
until well mixed. Add the nuts and blend again to thoroughly mix.

Pour batter into a greased loaf pan and bake at 350° for
50 to 60 minutes.

Peanut Butter Bread

1 cup all-purpose flour
½ cup quick cooking oats

½ cup cornmeal
½ cup dry milk powder
½ cup sugar
3 tsp. baking powder
1 tsp. salt
⅔ cup peanut butter
1 egg
1½ cups milk

In a large mixing bowl, combine the first 7 ingredients. Cut in peanut butter until it resembles coarse cornmeal.

Blend together the egg and milk and add to the flour mixture. Mix well.

Pour batter into a greased and floured loaf pan, making sure to spread the batter evenly. Bake at 325 ° for 1 hour and 10 minutes or until done. Remove from oven, let bread rest in the pan for 10 minutes, and then turn loaf out of the pan and onto a rack to continue cooling.

Pumpkin Bread

3 cups brown sugar
5 cups whole wheat flour
1 tsp. cinnamon
½ tsp. cloves
1 tsp. salt
1 slightly heaping T. baking soda
1 cup oil
2½ cups canned pumpkin
2 eggs, beaten

Mix together dry ingredients, add the oil, pumpkin, and eggs, and then blend thoroughly. Divide batter between 2 greased loaf pans.

Bake at 350° for about 1 hour and 20 minutes or until done.

Sour Cream Corn Bread

¾ cup cornmeal
1 cup flour
¼ cup sugar
2 tsp. baking powder
½ tsp. baking soda
¾ tsp. salt
1 cup sour cream
¼ cup milk
1 egg, beaten
2 T. butter or shortening, melted

Mix together all ingredients just until moistened. Pour batter into a greased 8-inch square pan and bake at 425° for 20 minutes or until done.

Walnut Bread with Streusel Filling

3 cups all-purpose flour
1 cup sugar
4 tsp. baking powder
2 tsp. salt
1 egg, beaten
¼ cup shortening, melted
1½ cups milk
1 tsp. vanilla
1½ cups walnuts, chopped
Streusel Filling (recipe follows)

Sift together the flour, sugar, baking powder, and salt. Add egg, shortening, milk, and vanilla and stir just until all the flour is moistened. Stir in walnuts.

Pour half of the batter into a greased 9 x 5 x 3-inch loaf pan. Sprinkle with Streusel Filling. Top with remaining batter and bake at 350° for about 1 hour and 20 minutes or until done.

Streusel Filling
⅓ cup brown sugar, packed
1½ T. flour
1 tsp. cinnamon
2 T. butter

Mix all ingredients together, breaking up butter until mixture resembles coarse peas.

Whole Wheat Quick Buttermilk Bread

1 qt. buttermilk
4 cups whole wheat flour
3 cups brown sugar
pinch of salt
1 tsp. baking soda

Mix together all ingredients and pour batter into 2 greased loaf pans. Bake at 350° for 60 to 70 minutes.

Zucchini Bread

3 cups all-purpose flour
1½ cups sugar
1 tsp. cinnamon
1 tsp. salt
1 tsp. baking powder
1 tsp. baking soda
2 cups zucchini, shredded
1 cup nuts, chopped
1 cup raisins
3 eggs, beaten
1 cup oil
cinnamon sugar

In a large bowl, stir together the dry ingredients. Add the zucchini, nuts, and raisins.

In a small bowl, mix together the eggs and oil and pour over the zucchini mixture. Stir until blended.

Pour into 2 loaf pans and sprinkle with cinnamon sugar. Bake at 350° for 40 to 45 minutes or until done.

BISCUITS AND MUFFINS

*Give her of the fruit of her hands; and let
her own works praise her in the gates.*

PROVERBS 31:31

Biscuits and muffins are a quick and easy addition to any meal, and they can be a healthful alternative to the more usual desserts and snacks. Many of these recipes freeze quite well for short periods, so by having some baked ahead and frozen, you and your loved ones have an edge on hectic mornings. Just grab a muffin, and you're on your way. Homemade fast food—and much better for you!

BISCUITS

Angel Biscuits

4½ tsp. (2 packages) active dry yeast
¼ cup warm water
2 cups warm buttermilk
5 cups all-purpose flour
⅓ cup sugar
2 tsp. salt
2 tsp. baking powder
1 tsp. baking soda
1 cup shortening
melted butter for brushing tops of baked biscuits

In a small bowl, mix together the yeast and warm water. Let set for 5 minutes. Stir in warm buttermilk. Set aside.

In a large bowl, mix together the flour, sugar, salt, baking powder, and baking soda. Cut in the shortening until mixture resembles coarse cornmeal. Stir in the yeast mixture.

Turn the dough out onto a lightly floured surface and knead gently 5 times. Roll out the dough to ½-inch thickness and cut with a biscuit cutter. Place biscuits on a lightly greased baking sheet, cover, and let rise until double, about 1½ hours.

Bake in a preheated 450° oven 8 to 10 minutes or until done. Remove from oven and immediately brush tops with melted butter.

Buttermilk Biscuits

2 cups all-purpose flour
½ tsp. salt
3 tsp. baking powder

½ tsp. baking soda
3 T. shortening
1 cup buttermilk

Sift together the flour, salt, baking powder, and baking soda. Cut in the shortening until the mixture resembles coarse crumbles. Add the buttermilk all at once and mix with a fork until it forms a ball. Turn out the dough onto a floured surface and knead for 30 seconds. Roll out the dough to ½-inch thickness and then cut with a biscuit cutter.

Place biscuits on an ungreased baking sheet and bake at 425° for 15 minutes.

- -

Cheesy Biscuits

2 cups all-purpose flour
¾ tsp. salt
3 tsp. baking powder
1 tsp. baking soda
4 T. shortening
1 cup shredded Cheddar cheese
1 cup buttermilk

Sift together the flour, salt, baking powder, and baking soda. Cut in the shortening until the mixture resembles coarse crumbles. Add cheese and stir to mix thoroughly. Add the buttermilk all at once and mix with a fork until it forms a ball. Turn out the dough onto a floured surface and knead for 30 seconds. Roll out dough to ½-inch thickness. Cut with a biscuit cutter and place biscuits on a greased baking sheet.

Bake at 425° for 15 minutes or until done.

Cream Scones

2 cups all-purpose flour
3 tsp. baking powder
2 T. plus 2 tsp. sugar, divided
½ tsp. salt
4 T. butter
2 eggs
⅓ cup whipping cream

In a large mixing bowl, sift together the flour, baking powder, 2 tablespoons sugar, and salt. Cut in the butter until mixture resembles coarse crumbs. Make a well in the center.

In a separate bowl, separate the yolk of one of the eggs (reserve the egg white to brush tops of scones) and stir the yolk together with the other whole egg and then stir in cream. Pour this mixture into the well and stir with a fork just until dough pulls away from the sides of the bowl.

Sprinkle a clean surface with a small amount of flour. Using your hands, pat the dough into a ball and knead it on the floured surface about 10 times. Divide dough ball into 2 equal halves. Roll out each half into a 1-inch-thick circle (it will be about 6 inches in diameter). Cut each circle into 4 pie-shaped wedges and place them on an ungreased baking sheet about 1 inch apart. Brush tops with the reserved egg white and then sprinkle the tops with the 2 teaspoons of sugar.

Bake in a preheated 400° oven 15 minutes. The scones are good plain but even better when topped with jam and sweetened whipped cream.

Crisp Biscuits

2 cups all-purpose flour
2 tsp. baking powder
1 tsp. salt
⅓ cup butter
¾ cup milk

Mix in the order given. Roll out to ¼-inch thickness. Cut into small rounds and bake on lightly greased baking sheet at 400° for 12 minutes.

Drop Biscuits

2 cups all-purpose flour
4 tsp. baking powder
½ tsp. salt
5 T. shortening
1 cup milk

Sift together the flour, baking powder, and salt into a bowl. Cut the shortening into the flour mixture until it resembles coarse cornmeal. Make a well in the center and pour in the milk all at once. Stir with a fork until well mixed. The dough will be quite soft.

Drop by heaping tablespoons onto a greased baking sheet and bake in a preheated 450° oven 15 to 20 minutes.

Herb Biscuits

2 cups all-purpose flour
2 tsp. baking powder
¼ tsp. baking soda
1 tsp. salt
¼ tsp. dry mustard
½ tsp. sage
½ tsp. celery seed
¼ cup shortening
¾ cup buttermilk

Mix together the dry ingredients and herbs. Cut in the shortening, add buttermilk, and stir to make a soft dough. Turn the dough out onto a lightly floured surface, knead lightly about 20 times, and roll to ½-inch thickness. Cut into biscuits and place on an ungreased baking sheet.

Bake at 425° for 10 minutes or until golden brown and done.

Lard Biscuits

2 cups all-purpose flour
4 tsp. baking powder
½ tsp. salt
3 T. lard
¾ cup milk

In a medium mixing bowl, mix together the flour, baking powder, and salt. Using a fork, cut in the lard until the mixture resembles coarse crumbles. Make a well in the middle and pour the milk into the well all at once. Mix with the fork until a soft dough forms. Then use one of your hands to gently knead the dough right in the bowl, about 10 to 15 times. Turn the dough out onto a lightly floured surface and roll to ½-inch thickness. Cut with a biscuit or cookie cutter and place the biscuits on a greased baking sheet.

Bake in a preheated 450° oven 12 minutes or until biscuits are light golden brown.

Light and Airy Biscuits

2 cups all-purpose flour
½ tsp. salt
2 tsp. sugar
4 tsp. baking powder
½ tsp. cream of tartar
½ cup shortening
⅔ cup milk

Sift together the flour, salt, sugar, baking powder, and cream of tartar. Cut in the shortening until the mixture resembles coarse cornmeal. Add the milk all at once and stir until the dough leaves the side of the bowl.

Roll out the dough to ½-inch thickness and cut with a biscuit cutter. Place biscuits on an ungreased baking sheet. Bake in a preheated 450° oven 15 minutes or until done.

Popovers

3 eggs
1 cup milk
3 T. melted butter
1 cup all-purpose flour
½ tsp. salt

Preheat oven to 375°. Grease eight 6-oz. custard cups and place them in a jelly roll pan.

In a large mixing bowl, beat eggs on low speed until frothy. Beat in the milk and butter. Gradually add the flour and salt to the egg mixture, beating until well combined and smooth.

Pour about ¾ cup of the batter into each of the 8 greased cups. Bake 50 minutes and then remove the pan from the oven and cut a small slit in the top of each popover to let out steam. Return to oven and bake an additional 10 minutes. Immediately remove popovers from custard cups and serve. They are good as is, but you can also serve them with pats of butter.

Savory Potato and Vegetable Scones

2½ to 3 cups all-purpose flour
1 T. plus 1 tsp. baking powder
1½ tsp. salt
4 oz. cream cheese
¼ cup Cheddar cheese, shredded
1 egg
1 cup cream
1 T. butter
¼ cup finely diced green, red, yellow, and/or orange
    bell peppers (Using multiple colors isn't necessary,
    but it makes the scones prettier.)
¼ cup onion, finely diced
½ large potato, peeled, cooked, and diced fine
⅛ cup fresh mushrooms, thinly sliced or diced
⅛ tsp. dried sage
⅛ tsp. dried rosemary

Preheat oven to 400°.

Mix together dry ingredients and set aside.

In a large bowl, cream together the cheeses and egg. Add cream and mix well.

On medium-low heat, sauté the vegetables in butter until soft, about 4 minutes. Add them to the cream mixture and stir well. Add the dry ingredients and stir by hand until a soft dough forms.

Pat out dough into a 1-inch-thick circle. Place the circle on a buttered cookie sheet and then using a pizza cutter or knife, cut it into 8 equal wedges (as if you were cutting pie).

Bake 20 to 25 minutes or until done. Remove scones from baking sheet and set on wire rack to cool.

Traditional Biscuits

2 cups all-purpose flour
4 tsp. baking powder
½ tsp. salt
⅓ cup shortening
¾ cup milk

In a bowl, sift together the flour, baking powder, and salt. Cut the shortening into the flour mixture until it is completely incorporated. Make a well in the center and pour the milk into the well all at once. Stir with a fork until the dough comes clean from the sides of the bowl.

Turn the dough out onto a lightly floured surface and knead it gently about 10 times. Roll or pat to ½-inch thickness and cut the biscuits using a biscuit cutter or the top of a glass. Place biscuits on an ungreased baking sheet about 1 inch apart. Bake in a preheated 450° oven 15 to 20 minutes.

MUFFINS

Bacon and Cheddar Cheese Muffins

2 cups all-purpose flour
2 T. sugar
3 tsp. baking powder
½ tsp. salt
½ cup cooked, crumbled bacon
½ cup Cheddar cheese
¼ cup finely diced sweet onions (optional)
1 cup milk
1 egg, beaten
4 T. butter, melted and cooled to lukewarm

In a large bowl, sift together the flour, sugar, baking powder, and salt. Add the bacon, cheese, and onion (if using) and mix again. Make a well in the center of the flour mixture.

In a small bowl, mix together the milk, egg, and melted butter. Mix well. Pour milk mixture all at once into the well and stir just until moistened. Batter will be lumpy.

Fill greased or paper-lined muffin tin cups ⅔ full and bake in a preheated 425° oven 20 to 25 minutes. Immediately remove muffins from pan and place on rack to cool.

Berry Muffins

1¾ cups all-purpose flour
1 cup plus 1 T. sugar, divided
2½ tsp. baking powder
½ tsp. cinnamon
¼ tsp. salt
1 cup milk

¼ cup butter, melted
1 egg, beaten
1 tsp. vanilla
1 cup berries (blueberries, blackberries, cranberries, etc.)

Grease muffin pans. Preheat oven to 375°.

In a large bowl, stir together the flour, 1 cup sugar, baking powder, cinnamon, and salt.

In another bowl, stir together milk, butter, egg, and vanilla. Add to the dry ingredients and stir just until blended. Batter will be lumpy. Fold in berries.

Fill prepared muffin cups ¾ full. Sprinkle with remaining sugar. Bake 20 minutes or until done.

Blueberry Oatmeal Muffins

1 cup all-purpose flour
2 tsp. baking powder
½ tsp. salt
½ tsp. cinnamon
½ cup brown sugar
¾ cup rolled oats
1 egg
1 cup milk
¼ cup butter, melted
¾ cup blueberries, fresh or frozen
sugar or cinnamon sugar for sprinkling

Stir together the flour, baking powder, salt, and cinnamon. Add the sugar and rolled oats and mix well.

In a large bowl, beat together the egg, milk, and butter. Add dry ingredients and stir until just moistened. Fold in blueberries.

Fill muffin tins about ⅔ full and sprinkle a bit of sugar on top of each muffin. Bake at 375° for 20 minutes or until done.

Bread Crumb Muffins

1 egg, beaten
1 cup milk
¼ cup butter, melted
1 cup dry bread crumbs
1 cup all-purpose flour
1 T. sugar
½ tsp. salt
1 T. baking powder

In a large mixing bowl, stir together the egg, milk, butter, and bread crumbs.

In another bowl, sift together the flour, sugar, salt, and baking powder. Add this to the milk mixture and stir just until moistened.

Fill greased muffin tin cups ⅔ full and bake at 375° for 25 minutes or until done.

Chocolate Chip Muffins

1½ cups all-purpose flour
½ cup sugar
2 tsp. baking powder
½ tsp. salt
1 egg
½ cup milk
¼ cup vegetable oil
¾ cup chocolate chips

Sift together the flour, sugar, baking powder, and salt. Beat the egg and add it to the flour mixture along with the milk and oil. Stir just until blended—don't overmix. Gently fold in the chocolate chips.

Fill greased muffin tins about ⅔ full. Bake in a preheated 400° oven 20 to 25 minutes or until done.

- -

Cornmeal Muffins

1 cup cornmeal
1 cup all-purpose flour
¼ cup sugar
1 tsp. salt
4 tsp. baking powder
1 cup milk
2 eggs, beaten
4 T. butter or shortening, melted

Sift together the dry ingredients and then add the milk, eggs, and butter. Stir the mixture just until the dry ingredients are moistened.

Fill greased muffin tin cups about ⅔ full and bake in a preheated 400° oven 20 minutes or until done.

- -

Four-Week Refrigerator Bran Muffins

6 cups ready-to-eat bran cereal, divided
2 cups boiling water
1 cup shortening or butter
1½ cups sugar
4 eggs
1 qt. buttermilk
5 cups all-purpose flour
5 tsp. baking soda
1 tsp. salt
raisins, dates, dried cranberries, or nuts (optional)

Place 2 cups bran cereal in a bowl and pour in the boiling water. Set aside to cool. Meanwhile, cream together the shortening or butter, sugar, and eggs. To this mixture, add the buttermilk and the cooled cereal mixture.

Sift together the flour, baking soda, and salt and add to the creamed mixture. Stir until the flour is moistened. Fold in an additional 4 cups *dry* bran cereal.

Store batter in a covered container in the refrigerator. Keeps up to 4 weeks.

When ready to bake muffins, preheat oven to 400° and fill well-greased muffin tin cups ⅔ full. Bake 20 minutes or until done. Note that the optional raisins, nuts, and dried fruit can be added to the muffin batter just before baking.

Fresh Peach Muffins

1 cup peeled and chopped fresh peaches
1 tsp. lemon juice
⅔ cup granulated sugar
½ tsp. salt
¼ tsp. cinnamon
3 tsp. baking powder
1 cup milk
1 egg
¼ cup butter, melted
2 cups all-purpose flour

In a small bowl, sprinkle peaches with lemon juice, mix to cover pieces, and set aside.

In another bowl, mix together the sugar, salt, cinnamon, and baking powder. Add the milk, egg, and butter and mix well. Add the flour and mix again. Fold in fruit and then fill greased muffin tins ⅔ full and bake at 450° for 20 minutes.

Ginger Muffins

¼ cup shortening
¼ cup sugar
1 egg
½ cup molasses
1½ cups all-purpose flour
¾ tsp. baking soda
¼ tsp. salt
½ tsp. cinnamon
½ tsp. ground ginger
¼ tsp. ground cloves
¼ cup bran
½ cup buttermilk

Cream together the shortening and sugar. Beat in egg and then molasses.

Sift together flour, baking soda, salt, cinnamon, ginger, cloves, and bran. Stir dry ingredients into molasses mixture. Gradually add buttermilk, beating until smooth.

Fill greased muffin tin cups ⅔ full and bake at 375° for 20 to 25 minutes.

Graham Muffins

1 cup graham or whole wheat flour
1 cup all-purpose flour
1 tsp. baking soda
¼ cup brown sugar
¼ tsp. salt
½ cup raisins (optional)
1 egg, beaten
1 cup buttermilk or sour milk
3 T. butter, melted

BISCUITS AND
MUFFINS

101

In a large mixing bowl, stir together the wheat and white flours, baking soda, brown sugar, salt, and raisins (optional).

In a smaller bowl, mix together the egg, buttermilk or sour milk, and the butter.

Make a well in the center of the flour mixture and pour the buttermilk mixture into the well. Stir just until blended.

Fill greased muffin tin cups half full and bake in a preheated 375° oven 15 minutes or until done.

Lemon Muffins

2 cups self-rising flour
1 box lemon pudding mix
2 T. sugar
1⅓ cups milk
¼ cup oil
powdered sugar

In a large bowl, sift together the flour, pudding mix, and sugar. Combine milk and oil and blend into the flour mixture, stirring just until moistened.

Fill greased muffin tin cups ⅔ full and bake at 425° for 20 to 25 minutes. Remove from oven and sprinkle with powdered sugar.

Oatmeal Muffins

1 cup rolled oats
1 cup milk
1 cup all-purpose flour
⅓ cup sugar
1 T. baking powder
½ tsp. salt

1 egg, well beaten
¼ cup oil

Combine the oats and milk and let stand for 15 minutes.

In the meantime, in a large bowl, sift together the flour, sugar, baking powder, and salt. Combine egg, oil, and oatmeal mixture. Add all at once to the dry ingredients and stir just until moistened.

Fill muffin tin cups ⅔ full and bake at 425° for 20 to 25 minutes or until done.

Sour Cream Muffins

1 egg
1 cup sour cream
2 T. butter, melted
2 cups all-purpose flour
¼ cup sugar
2 tsp. baking powder
½ tsp. baking soda
½ tsp. salt
¼ cup milk

Beat egg and sour cream until light and fluffy. Add butter, sifted dry ingredients, and milk. Stir just until dry ingredients are moistened. Fill greased muffin tin cups half full and bake at 400° for 20 minutes or until done.

Whole Wheat Muffins

2 cups whole wheat flour
4 tsp. baking powder
1 tsp. salt
2 T. sugar
1 cup milk
2 T. butter or shortening, melted

Mix together the flour, baking powder, salt, and sugar. Make a well in the center and stir in the milk and butter until thoroughly blended together.

Fill greased muffin tin cups ⅔ full and bake in a preheated 425° oven 20 to 25 minutes or until done.

Whole Wheat Pineapple Muffins

1 cup whole wheat flour
1 cup all-purpose flour
3 tsp. baking powder
½ tsp. salt
¼ cup sugar
¼ cup butter
1 egg
1 cup crushed pineapple, undrained

In a large mixing bowl, sift together the wheat and all-purpose flours, baking powder, and salt.

In a medium bowl, cream together the sugar and butter until fluffy. Add the egg and beat well again. Stir in the pineapple.

Pour the pineapple mixture into the dry ingredients and stir just enough to moisten the flour.

Fill greased muffin tin cups ⅔ full and bake in a preheated 400° oven 15 to 20 minutes or until done. Remove baked muffins from the tin at once.

DOUGHNUTS AND SWEET ROLLS

She looketh well to the ways of her household,
and eateth not the bread of idleness.

PROVERBS 31:27

Doughnuts, cinnamon rolls, and the like can seem daunting, and even those of us who are comfortable baking bread might hesitate when it comes to tackling the recipes in this chapter. But fear not. They aren't difficult—but they do require a good amount of time and effort to prepare. These are recipes that you'll want to bake for special occasions. And when your family and friends sink their teeth into these freshly homemade doughnuts or something equally tasty, they will be amazed at your obvious skill as a baker and fondly and gratefully remember those moments spent together eating.

A Word About Frying Doughnuts

A deep-fat fryer is nice to have mainly because it "watches" the temperature for you—just set the dial and you're good to go. But there's no need to run out and buy one. In fact, I no longer use a deep-fat fryer. Instead, I use a deep-sided cast iron pot, and it works very well. Here are some tips that will ensure your success as well.

- Heat the oil to 375°. I use a thermometer to take a reading, and anything above 350° seems to work fine. But don't go over 375° or you'll have scorching and smoking problems.

- When you're frying doughnuts, resist the urge to crowd them in the fryer. They need room to puff up a bit and grow, and if you put too many in at one time, the temperature will lower too much.

- Fry doughnuts about 2 minutes on each side. The time may vary slightly depending on how thick the doughnuts are, but this is a good benchmark.

- Use a long-handled metal spatula to slide the doughnuts into the fryer. You can use the spatula to turn them also.

- Long-handled tongs work even better for turning. Use the tongs or a long wooden knitting needle, thin dowel, or chopstick to grab the doughnuts through their holes to remove them from the fryer. You can remove doughnut holes with the tongs or a large stainless steel slotted spoon.

- Allow the doughnuts to drip fat into the fryer for several seconds and then place them on several layers of paper towels, turning the doughnuts so both sides are blotted.

- Once the doughnuts cool, you can cover them with frosting or sugar. I like to carefully shake the doughnuts in a paper bag or plastic baggie partially filled with sugar to evenly coat them.

- Doughnuts are best eaten the day they are made, but if you plan on keeping them for a day or so, cover them well and keep them at room temperature.

Apple Fritters

2 cups cake flour
2 T. sugar
1½ tsp. baking powder
½ tsp. salt
2 eggs, beaten
⅔ cup milk
3 T. butter, melted
½ tsp. vanilla
2 T. lemon juice or orange juice
1½ cups peeled, chopped apples
oil for frying
sugar or cinnamon sugar

In a large bowl, combine the flour, sugar, baking powder, and salt. In another bowl, mix together the eggs, milk, butter, vanilla, and lemon juice. Add to the dry ingredients and mix just until thoroughly moistened. Fold in apples.

Drop a tablespoonful into hot oil measuring at least ½-inch deep. You can use a deep-fat fryer, but a cast iron pot works just as well. When the first side is golden brown, turn the fritter and fry the second side. The fritters will probably take about 2 to 3 minutes on each side, but check the first batch to make sure they're done and then time subsequent batches accordingly.

Drain on paper towels and then sprinkle the fritters with sugar or cinnamon sugar while they are still warm.

Bismarcks

3 to 3½ cups all-purpose flour, divided
2¼ tsp. (1 package) active dry yeast
¼ cup sugar
1 tsp. salt

¾ cup milk
¼ cup water
¼ cup shortening
1 egg
¼ cup jam or jelly of your choice
oil for frying

In a large mixing bowl, combine 1½ cups flour, yeast, sugar, and salt and mix well.

In a saucepan, heat together the milk, water, and shortening until warm (about 120°). Shortening won't be entirely melted, but that's okay. Add to flour mixture. Add the egg, blend, and then beat at medium speed for 3 minutes. By hand, gradually stir in enough remaining flour to make a soft dough. Turn out dough onto a lightly floured surface and knead 5 to 8 minutes. Place the dough in a large greased bowl, turning dough so all surfaces are greased. Cover with a towel and let rise until double, about 1 to 1½ hours.

Punch down dough. Divide into 2 equal parts. On a lightly floured surface, roll out each half to a 12 x 6-inch rectangle. Using a biscuit cutter, cut dough into 2½-inch circles or squares. Place on floured cookie sheets and let rise until double, about 30 to 45 minutes.

Heat oil to 375° and fry the bismarcks until golden brown on both sides. Drain on paper towels and then cool. Cut a 1-inch slit in the side of each bismarck and spoon ½ teaspoon jam or jelly into the slit. Press the slit edge gently to close.

Blackberry Cheese Roll

2 cups all-purpose flour
4 tsp. baking powder
½ tsp. salt
¼ cup butter, chilled

1 cup shredded Cheddar cheese
¾ cup milk
2½ cups fresh or frozen blackberries
½ cup plus 2 T. sugar
¼ cup brown sugar
½ tsp. nutmeg
heavy cream or sweetened whipped cream

In a large mixing bowl, stir together the flour, baking powder, and salt. Add the butter and cut it into the flour mixture until it resembles coarse crumbs. Stir in the cheese and then the milk. Don't overmix. With as light a touch as possible, roll the dough out to a 10 x 12-inch rectangle about ⅓-inch thick. Sprinkle the blackberries evenly over the top and then do the same with ½ cup of the sugar, the brown sugar, and nutmeg.

Starting from a long edge, roll up dough jelly-roll style and transfer the roll to a greased baking sheet, seam side down. Pinch the ends to seal and tuck the ends underneath the roll. Sprinkle with the remaining 2 tablespoons of sugar and bake in a preheated 350° oven 45 minutes or until done. Slice and serve warm with heavy cream or sweetened whipped cream.

Caramel Apple Dumplings

2 cups brown sugar
3 cups water
¼ tsp. cinnamon
½ tsp. nutmeg
2 cups all-purpose flour
1 tsp. salt
2 tsp. baking powder
¾ cup shortening
¼ cup butter
½ cup milk
6 apples, peeled and cored

In a saucepan, mix together the brown sugar, water, cinnamon, and nutmeg. Turn to medium high and while stirring, bring the mixture to a boil and boil for 10 minutes. Remove from heat and set aside.

Mix together the flour, salt, and baking powder. Cut in the shortening and butter until mixture resembles coarse crumbs. Stir in the milk and mix well to form a soft dough. Cut the dough into 6 equal pieces. Roll out each piece of dough into the shape of a circle. Wrap each of the apples with a dough circle. Place the wrapped apples on a baking pan with sides and pour the sauce over the apples.

Bake in a preheated 375° oven 35 minutes or until the apples are cooked through.

Chocolate Baking Powder Doughnuts

2 cups all-purpose flour
½ cup unsweetened cocoa powder
2½ tsp. baking powder
½ tsp. baking soda
¼ tsp. salt
¼ tsp. cinnamon (optional)
1½ T. butter, softened
¾ cup sugar
1 egg
½ cup milk
oil for frying

Mix together the flour, cocoa powder, baking powder, baking soda, salt, and cinnamon (optional).

In a separate large bowl, cream together the butter and sugar. Beat in the egg and mix well. Alternately add flour mixture and milk, mixing well after each addition.

Turn out onto a floured surface, roll ¼-inch thick, and cut into small doughnuts (about 2 inches in diameter).

Fry in oil, turning once and being careful not to crowd the doughnuts while cooking. Drain on paper towels. When cooled, frost the doughnuts or sprinkle them with powdered sugar.

- -

Cinnamon Fans

3 cups all-purpose flour
1 tsp. salt
4 tsp. baking powder
1 tsp. cream of tartar
⅓ cup sugar
¾ cup shortening
1 cup milk

Filling
½ cup butter, melted and cooled
½ cup sugar
2 T. cinnamon

Stir together dry ingredients. Cut in shortening until the mixture resembles coarse crumbs. Add milk and stir. On a floured surface, knead dough gently for a half minute. Roll dough into the shape of a rectangle about ¼-inch thick. (The rectangle should be about 8 x 24 inches.)

Spread the melted butter, sugar, and cinnamon over the top of the dough for the filling. Cut dough the long way into four 2-inch-wide strips. Then stack the 4 strips on top of one another and cut the stack into 2-inch-wide pieces. Turn the pieces on their sides in greased muffin tin cups so each treat fans out.

Bake at 400° for 12 minutes or until golden brown.

Cinnamon Rolls

⅓ cup butter
1 can evaporated milk
¾ cup sugar
3 T. active dry yeast
3 eggs
1 T. salt
4 cups all-purpose flour (plus more as needed)

Filling
¾ cup butter, softened
2 to 3 cups sugar
cinnamon
Raisins and nuts (optional)

In a small saucepan, gently heat the butter and evaporated milk just until barely warm. Don't let the mixture get too hot.

In a large mixing bowl, mix together the evaporated milk mixture, sugar, and yeast. Let rest for 5 minutes. Add the eggs 1 at a time, mixing well after each addition. Add the salt and mix well again. Slowly add the flour, mixing well as you add. Continue adding flour until the dough leaves the sides of the bowl and begins to ball up.

Turn out dough onto a lightly floured surface and knead for 10 minutes, using as little flour as possible to keep the dough from sticking. Place the dough ball in a large greased bowl, turning dough so entire surface is greased. Cover with a clean towel and let rise until double.

On a floured surface, roll out dough into a rectangle shape and spread with the filling ingredients in the order given. Roll dough into a log, starting at a long side. Cut into about 2 dozen rolls. Place rolls cut side up on 2 greased jelly roll pans, cover with a towel, and let rise again.

Bake in a preheated 350° oven 25 minutes or until done.

Cream Sticks

4½ tsp. (2 packages) active dry yeast
1 cup warm water
1 cup milk, scalded and then cooled
½ cup butter
⅔ cup sugar
2 eggs
½ tsp. salt
1 tsp. vanilla
6 cups all-purpose flour
oil for frying

Cream Filling
3 T. all-purpose flour
1 cup milk
1 cup sugar
1 cup shortening
1 tsp. vanilla
2½ cups powdered sugar

Frosting
½ cup brown sugar
4 T. butter
2 T. milk
1 tsp. vanilla
powdered sugar

Dissolve yeast in warm water and let it sit until bubbly, about 10 minutes. Mix in the remaining ingredients, stirring as you go. Add enough flour to make a soft dough. Cover the bowl and let the dough rise until double. Punch down and turn out onto a lightly floured surface and gently knead for several minutes. Form into bars, each about 3½ x 1½ inches. Cover and let them rise again. Fry in deep fat.

To make the cream filling, mix together the flour and milk and heat in a saucepan, stirring constantly until thickened. Set aside to cool.

In a medium bowl, cream together the sugar and short-ening. Add the milk and flour mixture and the vanilla. Mix well. Add the powdered sugar a little bit at a time, mixing well each time.

Slit open the bars and fill with the cream filling.

To make the frosting, place the brown sugar, butter, and milk in a saucepan. Heat on low heat until the mixture begins to simmer. Continue cooking and stirring until it thickens. Set aside and allow the mixture to cool. Once cooled, add the vanilla and enough powdered sugar to make a spreadable frosting. Frost cream-filled bars.

Doughnuts for a Crowd

1 T. active dry yeast, slightly heaping
1½ cups sugar, divided
2 cups warm water
1 cup milk, scalded and then cooled to lukewarm
¾ cup cream
5 eggs, beaten
½ cup butter
½ tsp. salt
9 to 10 cups all-purpose flour, more or less

Dissolve yeast and ½ cup of the sugar in the warm water and scalded, cooled milk. Let the mixture sit for 15 minutes.

Add cream, beaten eggs, butter, the remaining cup of sugar, and salt and stir well to combine. Begin adding flour—enough to make a moderately stiff dough. Cover the dough with a clean towel and let the dough rise until double.

Punch down dough and roll out dough to ½- to ¾-inch thickness. Cut with a doughnut cutter and carefully place doughnuts (about 50) on very lightly floured trays. Cover them and let them rise again until double.

Fry doughnuts in shortening or oil and drain on paper towels. If desired, frost or sprinkle them with powdered sugar, cinnamon sugar, or white sugar.

- -

Easy Cinnamon Rolls

¾ cup milk
¾ cup water
½ cup shortening
½ cup sugar
2 eggs
2 tsp. salt
4½ tsp. (2 packages) active dry yeast, dissolved in ½
    cup lukewarm water
7 cups all-purpose flour, more or less
½ cup melted butter
cinnamon and sugar mixture

Sugar Glaze (optional)
1½ cups powdered sugar
2 to 3 T. water

Heat milk and water together until scalded. Cool to lukewarm.

Mix together shortening, sugar, eggs, and salt. Add milk mixture and stir well. Add dissolved yeast and stir well again. Add enough of the flour so the dough pulls away from the sides of the bowl. Turn out dough ball onto a floured surface and add the remaining flour as needed to keep dough from sticking as you knead for 5 minutes.

Place dough in a large greased bowl, turning dough ball so entire surface is greased. Cover with a towel and let rise until double in bulk, about 1 hour. Roll dough out to ¼-inch thickness. Cut with a biscuit cutter. Roll each piece out so it's long and thin. Dip in melted butter and then dredge in the cinnamon and sugar mixture. Roll each piece up and place on baking sheets with their sides not quite touching. Let rise about 30 to 45 minutes, and then place in a preheated 350° oven and bake 15 minutes or until done.

If desired, make Sugar Glaze by mixing powdered sugar and water together until well blended and a desired consistency. Drizzle over cooled cinnamon rolls.

Fastnachts

2 cups milk
½ cup shortening
¾ cup sugar
1 tsp. salt
2 eggs
2¼ tsp. (1 package) active dry yeast
2 T. warm water
7 cups all-purpose flour, more or less
oil for frying
powdered sugar

Heat the milk and shortening in a large saucepan to just below the boiling point. Turn off heat, stir in sugar and salt, and cool to lukewarm. Beat eggs and add to the milk mixture.

Dissolve the yeast in warm water. Let stand until slightly bubbly (about 10 minutes) and then add to the milk mixture.

Sift and then measure the flour, adding as much flour as needed to form a soft dough that can be handled easily. Knead the dough for 5 minutes. Wrap and place dough in the refrigerator overnight.

In the morning, roll out the dough to ¼-inch thickness and cut into 2-inch squares. Make a slit in the center of each square. Cover with a towel and let rise for about 45 minutes.

Fry in deep fat until golden brown, turning once so both sides are golden. While still warm, roll or gently shake in powdered sugar.

- -

Fattigman

12 to 13 cardamom seeds (1-2 pods)*
4 T. whipping cream
4 eggs
4 T. sugar
3¾ to 4 cups cake flour, sifted
oil for frying

Prepare seeds by removing pods and crushing very fine. Place in cream to soak.

Beat eggs until light and frothy and then add in the sugar. Beat again thoroughly. Add the cream and seed mixture and beat well again. Add the cake flour to make a dough stiff enough to roll very thin.

Roll out dough as thin as possible on a lightly floured surface. Cut the dough into squares or diamonds and slash each center twice to aid in quick cooking.

Fry the dough pieces in hot shortening or oil heated to 375° to 400° until they are faintly golden. The quicker these fry, the better—thin and crisp is the goal. Drain on towels that have been sprinkled with powdered sugar. When cool enough to handle, shake fattigman pieces with powdered sugar in a paper bag.

These keep well in a tightly closed container.

* You can sometimes find cardamom seeds, and this will save the step of cracking the pods. However, cardamom is the most flavorful when the seeds are ground from freshly cracked pods. Yes, it's fiddly but so worth the effort!

German Rolls

4½ cups all-purpose flour, divided
1 tsp. salt
1 cup white sugar
1 tsp. baking soda
2 tsp. cream of tartar
½ cup lard or shortening
½ cup butter
2 eggs
¼ cup milk
¼ cup water
1 cup brown sugar

In a large mixing bowl, sift together 4 cups of the flour, salt, white sugar, baking soda, and cream of tartar. Cut in lard and butter until mixture resembles coarse crumbs. Add 1 well-beaten egg, milk, and water and mix to form a soft dough.

In another bowl, mix together 1 beaten egg, brown sugar, and ½ cup flour.

Roll dough to ½-inch thickness and spread with the brown sugar mixture. Roll up like a jelly roll and cut into inch-thick slices. Place slices 2 inches apart on greased baking sheets.

Bake at 375° for 8 to 10 minutes.

Glazed Doughnuts

2¼ tsp. (1 package) yeast
1 cup warm water
1 cup mashed potatoes
1 cup lard or shortening
1 cup milk, scalded and cooled to lukewarm
½ cup sugar
2 eggs
all-purpose flour
oil for frying

Powdered Sugar Glaze
1 lb. (about 4 cups) powdered sugar
½ cup water

Dissolve yeast in warm water and let sit for 5 minutes. Add the mashed potatoes, lard, scalded (and cooled) milk, sugar, and eggs. Begin adding flour and stirring by hand. Add just enough flour so the dough doesn't stick to your fingers but is still soft (somewhere around 4-5 cups). Cover and let rise until double.

Roll out dough to ½- to ¾-inch thickness. Cut with a doughnut cutter and carefully place doughnuts on trays that have been lightly dusted with flour. Let rise for 30 minutes.

Fry doughnuts in hot shortening or oil, being careful not to crowd them. Drain for a moment on paper towels and then dip them in Powdered Sugar Glaze. Thread them onto a stick placed over the bowl of glaze so excess glaze falls back into the bowl to be reused.

To make Powdered Sugar Glaze, mix powdered sugar and water together, adding a bit more water if necessary to make desired consistency.

DOUGHNUTS AND SWEET ROLLS

Jelly Doughnuts

1 cup warm water
4½ tsp. (2 packages) active dry yeast
4½ cups all-purpose flour, divided
⅔ cup sugar
1 tsp. salt
⅔ cup butter, softened
3 eggs
2 tsp. vanilla
½ to ¾ cup jam or jelly of your choice
1 egg white, beaten
powdered sugar for dusting

In a large bowl, combine the warm water and yeast and let sit for 5 minutes. Add one cup of the flour and beat until smooth. Cover bowl and let batter rest for 30 minutes.

Add the sugar, salt, butter, eggs, and vanilla and beat again until smooth. Gradually add the remaining flour (about 3½ cups), beating with a wooden spoon until the dough pulls away from the sides of the bowl and is smooth. Cover with a clean towel and let rise until double, about 2 hours. Punch down dough and allow to rise until double again.

Roll out dough to ⅛-inch thickness and cut out doughnut rounds using a biscuit cutter. Lay out half of the doughnut rounds on a lightly floured surface and spoon 1 teaspoon jam onto the center of each. Paint the edge of each doughnut round with the egg white and then lay the other half of the doughnut rounds on top of the filled bottom. Pinch the edges together well to seal. Cover the doughnuts with a towel and let rise for 1 hour. Use an oiled spatula to pick up the doughnuts and place them in the fryer. Fry the doughnuts in hot shortening or oil for 2 to 3 minutes on each side or until done, and then set them on paper towels to drain. When cool, dust with powdered sugar.

Knee Patches

3 eggs
1 tsp. vanilla
2 tsp. salt
1 cup heavy cream
4 cups all-purpose flour
vegetable oil for frying
powdered sugar for sprinkling
cinnamon sugar for sprinkling (optional)

(Note that Knee Patches are also known as *Elephant Ears*.)

In a large mixing bowl, beat the eggs until frothy. Add the vanilla, salt, and cream and mix until well blended. Gradually add the flour and beat thoroughly. Because the dough will be stiff, consider using a large wooden spoon. Turn out dough onto a floured surface and knead for 10 minutes.

Preheat about 2 quarts oil to 375° in a deep-fat fryer or deep cast iron pot. Pinch off small pieces of dough about the size of a small walnut and roll out to shape a 4-inch circle. Now comes the fun part! Sit down and cover one of your knees with a clean tea towel. Lay the rolled-out dough on the towel and stretch the dough over your kneecap, working the dough until it's very thin.

Deep fry the knee patches in the hot oil for about 2 minutes per side. The knee patches will puff as they cook. Remove them carefully from the oil and lay them on paper towels to drain. Sprinkle the knee patches with powdered sugar or cinnamon sugar and eat while warm and fresh.

Long Johns

4½ tsp. (2 packages) active dry yeast
4 to 4½ cups all-purpose flour
¼ cup sugar
1 tsp. salt
½ tsp. nutmeg
½ cup water
½ cup light cream (half-and-half)
¼ cup shortening
1 egg
oil for frying

Maple Frosting
½ cup brown sugar, packed
¼ cup butter
¼ tsp. maple flavoring
2 T. light cream (half-and-half)
1 cup powdered sugar

In a large mixing bowl, combine yeast, 1½ cups of the flour, sugar, salt, and nutmeg and mix well.

In a saucepan, heat together the water, light cream, and shortening until warm but not hot. Note that the shortening will not be entirely melted. Add to the flour mixture. Add egg and blend at low speed until moistened, and then beat at medium speed for 3 minutes.

By hand, gradually stir in enough remaining flour to make a soft dough. Turn out onto a floured surface and knead until smooth, about 5 to 8 minutes. Place dough ball into a greased bowl, turning dough so entire surface is greased. Cover and let rise until double, about 1 hour.

Punch down dough and divide into 2 parts. Roll or pat out each piece to a 12 x 6-inch rectangle. Cut into 1-inch strips (each piece will be 6 inches long by 1 inch wide). Cover and let rise until double, about 30 to 45 minutes.

Fry the dough in hot shortening or oil, turning once, until golden brown. Drain on paper towels. When cool, frost with Maple Frosting or your favorite frosting or glaze or simply sprinkle with sugar.

To make Maple Frosting, mix together the brown sugar and butter in a small saucepan. Heat to boiling while stirring constantly. Boil for 2 minutes. Remove from heat and immediately stir in maple flavoring and light cream. Stir in enough powdered sugar until the frosting has a spreadable consistency.

Maple Bars

3 tsp. active dry yeast
¼ cup warm water
½ cup boiling water
½ cup shortening
⅓ cup sugar
1 tsp. salt
½ cup milk
2 eggs, beaten
5 to 6 cups all-purpose flour
oil for frying

Maple Glaze
3 cups powdered sugar
¼ tsp. maple extract (use a bit more if you like a strong
    maple flavor)
½ cup milk

Dissolve yeast in warm water.

In a large bowl, combine the boiling water, shortening, sugar, and salt and stir the mixture until it is lukewarm. Blend in the dissolved yeast, milk, and eggs. Gradually stir in enough flour until the dough leaves the sides of the bowl and is easy to handle. Turn out dough onto a floured surface and knead about 5 minutes. Place ball of dough into a greased bowl, turning ball of dough so the entire surface is greased. Cover and let rise until double, about 1 hour.

Turn the dough out onto a floured surface and roll it out to a ½-inch thickness. Cut into strips, the size of which pleases you, and place the strips on trays. Cover the strips and let rise until double (around 30 minutes).

Deep fry the strips, drain them on paper towels or other absorbent paper, and dip the tops in the Maple Glaze.

To make Maple Glaze, whisk all ingredients together until smooth.

- -

Moist Doughnuts

2¼ tsp. (1 package) active dry yeast
1 cup warm water
1 cup mashed potatoes
1 cup lard or shortening
1 cup milk, scalded and cooled to lukewarm
½ cup sugar
2 eggs, beaten
4 cups all-purpose flour, more or less
oil for frying

Dissolve yeast in warm water and let sit until bubbly, about 10 minutes. Add mashed potatoes, lard, milk, sugar, and eggs and mix well. Do your best to break up the lard into small pieces. Begin adding flour, mixing as you go. Add just enough flour so the dough begins to leave the sides of the bowl. Turn dough out on a floured surface and knead for several minutes, adding just enough remaining flour to make the dough not stick to your hands. Cover and let rise until double in bulk.

Roll out to ¼-inch thickness and cut doughnuts and holes using a doughnut cutter. Put on lightly floured trays, cover, and let rise again.

Fry doughnuts and holes in deep fat and then drain on paper towels. While doughnuts are still hot, dip each in a thin glaze made from 4 cups powdered sugar mixed with ½ cup water. You can also cool the doughnuts and then frost or sprinkle them with sugar.

- -

Old-Fashioned Sour Cream Doughnuts

2¼ cups all-purpose flour
1½ tsp. baking powder
1 tsp. salt
½ tsp. nutmeg (optional)
½ cup sugar
2 T. lard, butter, or shortening
2 egg yolks
⅔ cup sour cream
oil for frying

Glaze
3½ cups powdered sugar
2 tsp. corn syrup
¼ tsp. salt
½ tsp. vanilla
½ cup hot water

In a medium bowl, combine the flour, baking powder, salt, and nutmeg. Set aside.

In a large mixing bowl and using an electric mixer, beat together the sugar and shortening for about 1 minute or until mixture resembles coarse sand. Add the egg yolks and mix until light, about 1 minute more. Add sour cream and mix well. Stir in flour mixture and mix until all ingredients are very well combined. Cover the bowl and set in the refrigerator for at least an hour or as long as overnight.

When ready to fry doughnuts, heat oil in a deep-fat fryer or heavy pot, making sure the oil is at least 2 inches deep. While oil is heating to 375°, roll out dough on a floured surface to about ½-inch thick. Use a doughnut cutter to cut out doughnuts and holes. Gently knead the left-over bits and pieces together to roll out and cut as many doughnuts as possible. Anything too small or misshapen can be fried as is—these odd shapes are sometimes called puppy dog tails!

Dust off as much flour as possible before sliding dough-nuts gently into the heated oil. Don't crowd them. Work in shifts to fry all the doughnuts as follows: When the doughnuts float to the top of the oil, fry another 15 sec-onds. Carefully flip them over and fry until they are golden brown and cracked, about 1½ minutes. Then flip them back over and finish frying the first side until they are golden brown and cracked also, about 1¼ minutes.

Set the doughnuts on a rack with paper towels under-neath to catch the drips. When they have cooled enough to handle, dip them in the glaze.

To make the glaze, whisk together all glaze ingredients until well blended and smooth. Dip the warm dough-nuts in the warm glaze and set them on racks to cool for about 10 minutes before eating.

Oven-Baked Doughnuts

4½ tsp. (2 packages) active dry yeast
¼ cup warm water
1½ cups milk, scalded and then cooled
½ cup sugar
1 tsp. salt
1 tsp. nutmeg (optional)
¼ tsp. cinnamon (optional)
2 eggs
⅓ cup shortening
4½ cups all-purpose flour
¼ cup butter, melted
cinnamon sugar or plain sugar

In a large mixing bowl, dissolve the yeast in the warm water. Let sit until bubbly, about 10 minutes. Add the milk, sugar, salt, nutmeg and cinnamon (optional), eggs, shortening, and 2 cups of the flour. Beat these ingredients with an electric mixer for 1 minute, scraping the sides of the bowl often. Stir in the remaining flour and mix until the batter is smooth. Cover and let rise in a warm place until double, about 1 hour.

Turn the dough out onto a well-floured surface and roll the dough around in the flour so all surfaces are covered. The dough will be soft to handle. With a floured rolling pin, gently roll the dough to a ½-inch thickness. With a floured biscuit or doughnut cutter, cut out doughnuts, lift them carefully with a spatula, and place them on a greased baking sheet 2 inches apart. Brush them with melted butter and let them rise until double, about 30 minutes.

Bake the doughnuts at 425° for 8 to 10 minutes or until they are golden brown. Remove from the oven and immediately brush them with melted butter and sprinkle with sugar.

Pecan Caramel Rolls

6½ to 7 cups all-purpose flour
4½ tsp. (2 packages) active dry yeast
¾ cup granulated sugar, divided
1½ tsp. salt
1 cup milk
1 cup water
¾ cup butter, softened
2 eggs
¼ cup brown sugar
1 T. cinnamon

Topping
⅔ cup butter
⅔ cup brown sugar, packed
6 T. corn syrup
⅔ cup chopped pecans

In a large mixing bowl, combine 3 cups of the flour, yeast, ½ cup of the granulated sugar, and the salt. Mix well.

In a saucepan, heat milk, water, and ½ cup of the butter until warm (about 120°). The butter won't be completely melted, but that's okay. Add to the flour mixture along with the eggs. Blend at low speed until moistened and then on medium speed for 3 more minutes. Gradually stir in enough of the remaining flour by hand to make a soft dough. Turn out dough onto a lightly floured surface and knead until smooth, about 5 to 8 minutes. Place the dough into a large greased bowl, turning so entire surface of dough is greased. Cover and let rise until double, about 1 to 1½ hours.

While dough is rising, in a small bowl, mix together ¼ cup of the granulated sugar, brown sugar, and cinnamon for the filling. Set aside.

To make topping, in a small saucepan, combine the butter, brown sugar, and corn syrup. Stir and heat on medium-low until blended and ingredients are melted.

Divide topping between 2 greased 9 x 13-inch cake pans. Sprinkle topping with pecans.

Punch down dough and divide into 2 equal pieces. On a lightly floured surface, roll or pat each half to form a 12 x 15-inch rectangle. Spread with the ¼ cup softened butter, dividing the butter equally between the 2 rectangles of dough. Sprinkle the cinnamon filling mixture on top of the dough, dividing the filling equally. Starting with a long side, roll up tightly. Pinch edge to seal. Cut each roll into 12 slices and place the slices on the topping in the pans, 12 slices to a pan. Cover and let rise until almost double, about 30 to 45 minutes.

Bake in a preheated 375° oven 20 to 25 minutes or until done. Remove the pans from the oven. Using oven mitts so you don't burn yourself, quickly cover the pans with aluminum foil, invert the pans onto racks, and cool for 1 minute. Remove the rolls from the pans. Allow the pecan caramel rolls to cool long enough before eating so the hot syrup doesn't burn your fingers.

DOUGHNUTS AND SWEET ROLLS

Pluckems

⅓ cup plus ¾ cup sugar, divided
⅓ cup butter plus more for dipping, melted
½ tsp. salt
1 cup scalded milk
2¼ tsp. (1 package) yeast
¼ cup warm water
3 eggs, beaten
3¾ cups all-purpose flour, more or less
½ cup ground nut meats, such as walnuts or pecans
3 tsp. cinnamon

In a large bowl, mix together ⅓ cup of the sugar, ⅓ cup of the butter, salt, and scalded milk. While it's cooling to lukewarm, dissolve yeast in warm water in a small bowl and let sit.

When the scalded milk mixture has cooled, add the yeast and water mixture and stir. Add eggs and stir again. Then begin adding flour to make a stiff batter. Cover and let rise until the mixture doubles in bulk. Punch it down, and let rise again.

In another bowl, mix together ¾ cup of the sugar, ground nut meats, and cinnamon.

Roll the dough into balls the size of walnuts, dip them into melted butter, and then roll each ball in the nut meats mixture. Pile the balls loosely in an ungreased angel food cake or Bundt cake pan. Cover and let rise for 30 minutes.

Preheat oven to 400°. Turn the oven down to 350° and put the cake pan in the oven. Bake 40 to 50 minutes or until done. When baking is complete, remove from oven and immediately turn the pan upside down on a serving platter and slide the pluckems out of the pan. When they have cooled enough so they don't burn fingers or mouths, pluck 'em and eat 'em.

Quick Sticky Buns

4½ to 5 cups all-purpose flour
4½ tsp. (2 packages) active dry yeast
⅓ cup sugar
1 tsp. salt
1 cup milk
½ cup water
⅓ cup butter
1 egg

Topping
½ cup butter

½ cup brown sugar
½ cup chopped nuts (walnuts, pecans, or hazelnuts are good choices)

In a large mixing bowl, mix together 2 cups of the flour, yeast, sugar, and salt.

In a saucepan, heat the milk, water, and butter until warm (about 120°). The butter won't be entirely melted, but this is okay. Add to the flour mixture along with the egg and beat at medium speed for 3 minutes. By hand, gradually stir in enough remaining flour to make a soft dough.

Turn out dough onto a lightly floured surface and knead for 3 to 5 minutes or until smooth and elastic. Place the dough into a large greased bowl, turning dough so entire surface is greased. Heat your oven on the lowest setting for 2 minutes and then turn the oven off. Cover the bowl of dough with a towel and then place it into the oven to rise for 15 minutes.

Meanwhile, prepare topping by combining butter and brown sugar in a small saucepan. Heat and stir until blended. Add the nuts and stir again. Spoon topping equally into 24 greased muffin tin cups.

When the dough has rested for 15 minutes, divide the dough into 4 equal parts and divide each of the 4 parts into 6 pieces (24 pieces total). Shape each piece into a smooth ball and place into the muffin cups. Cover with a towel and let rise in the still-warm oven 10 minutes. Remove muffin tins from the oven and preheat the oven to 400°. Place the muffin tins back into the preheated oven and bake 10 minutes. Remove from the oven, cover the muffin tins with aluminum foil, and invert them onto racks. Cool for 1 minute before removing pans. Allow the sticky buns to cool enough so that the hot syrup doesn't burn your fingers when you eat them.

Rhubarb Dumplings

Sauce
1½ cups sugar
1 T. all-purpose flour
¼ tsp. cinnamon, generous
¼ tsp. salt
1½ cups water
⅓ cup butter
1 tsp. vanilla
red food coloring (optional)

Dough
2 cups all-purpose flour
2 T. sugar
2 tsp. baking powder
¼ tsp. salt
2½ T. butter, chilled
½ to ¾ cup milk

Filling
2 T. butter, room temperature
2 cups finely chopped rhubarb, fresh or frozen
½ cup sugar
ground cinnamon

To make sauce, in a small saucepan combine the sugar, flour, cinnamon, and salt. Gradually mix in the water. Add the butter and then bring to a boil over high heat and boil for 1 minute. Add the vanilla and food coloring if desired (using as many drops as you prefer to get a pleasing red color). Set aside and let cool.

To make the dough, in a medium mixing bowl stir together the flour, sugar, baking powder, and salt. Cut in the butter until the mixture resembles coarse crumbles. Add the milk and mix just until blended (don't overmix). Shape the dough into a ball and then turn out onto a floured surface. Roll out to form a 12 x 10-inch rectangle.

Spread the rectangle of dough with the softened butter and evenly spread rhubarb on top. Sprinkle sugar over all and dust with cinnamon. Roll up from the long side jelly-roll style. With the seam side down and using a sharp knife, cut the roll into 12 equal slices. Arrange them cut side up (like you would with cinnamon rolls) in a 9 x 13-inch, greased glass baking dish with sides. Pour cooled sauce over the dumplings and bake in a preheated 350° oven 35 minutes or until the dumplings look done and are puffy and golden brown. These are good served plain or with sweetened whipped cream or vanilla ice cream.

Soft Sugar Doughnuts

1 cup milk
2¼ tsp. (1 package) active dry yeast
3½ cups sifted all-purpose flour
¼ cup shortening
1 tsp. salt
¼ cup sugar
1 egg
oil for frying
sugar

Heat milk to lukewarm. Add yeast and stir to help dissolve. Add 1½ cups of the flour and beat until smooth, about 2 minutes. Cover and let rise until double, about 2 hours.

In another bowl, cream together the shortening, salt, and sugar. Add the egg and blend well. Stir into the yeast mixture. Add remaining flour, mixing as you go. Using a stand mixer if you have one or beating well by hand, beat for 5 minutes. Rub the top of the dough with shortening, cover bowl, and let rise again until double.

Roll out to ½-inch thickness and cut out doughnuts using a floured doughnut cutter. Transfer doughnuts to lightly floured trays and allow to rise for 45 minutes.

Fry doughnuts in hot oil, turning once, until done (about 3 to 5 minutes). Drain on paper towels. Let cool before sprinkling with sugar.

Sour Cream Buttermilk Doughnuts

½ cup sour cream
½ cup buttermilk
1 cup sugar
3 eggs, beaten
1 tsp. vanilla
4 cups all-purpose flour
2 tsp. baking powder
½ tsp. baking soda
½ tsp. salt
oil for frying
powdered sugar, granulated sugar, or cinnamon sugar

In a large bowl, beat together the sour cream and buttermilk until thoroughly mixed and smooth. Add the sugar and beat again until smooth. Add the eggs and vanilla and mix together thoroughly.

In another bowl, mix together the flour, baking powder, baking soda, and salt. Gradually add the flour mixture to the liquid ingredients, mixing just enough to make a sticky dough. Cover bowl and refrigerate 2 to 3 hours.

Turn out dough onto a well-floured surface and knead for about 3 minutes or until smooth. Roll dough out to a ½-inch thickness and cut out doughnuts using a floured doughnut cutter.

Fry in hot oil (375°) for 3 minutes. Turn doughnuts and fry the second side for 3 minutes or until golden brown. (When you fry doughnut holes, they tend to puff out sideways, so you'll need to turn them also. They may not take quite as long to fry golden brown as the doughnuts.) Drain doughnuts and holes and then sprinkle with powdered sugar, regular sugar, or cinnamon sugar.

DOUGHNUTS
AND SWEET ROLLS

COOKIES

Pleasant words are as an honeycomb, sweet
to the soul, and health to the bones.

Proverbs 16:24

Is there anything more welcoming than the smell of fresh-baked chocolate chip cookies as you walk into a home? Cookies are one of the ways we like to show love, whether we're baking them up for an after-school treat or a late-night snack. In this chapter, you'll find classic standbys as well as fancier treats for special occasions. And if you don't want to bake up the whole batch, be sure to pop the rest of the dough in the freezer so you can have hot, oven-fresh cookies at a moment's notice!

Amish Nut Balls

⅔ cup butter
1 cup ground nuts
1 cup all-purpose flour
3 T. sugar
1 tsp. vanilla
⅛ tsp. salt
½ cup powdered sugar

Preheat oven to 375°. Combine butter, ground nuts, flour, sugar, vanilla, and salt in a large mixing bowl. Work with fingers until well blended. Shape into balls the size of large marbles and place on ungreased cookie sheet. Bake 10 minutes. While still warm, roll in powdered sugar.

Apple Butter Cookies

½ cup unsalted butter
½ cup sugar
1 egg
½ cup apple butter
1 tsp. vanilla
1½ cups all-purpose flour
¼ tsp. salt
1 cup chopped pecans

Preheat oven to 350°. Cream butter and sugar. Mix in egg, apple butter, and vanilla. Stir in flour and salt until well combined. Fold in pecans. Roll into 1-inch balls and place on ungreased cookie sheets. Bake 12 to 15 minutes. Let cool on cookie sheet 5 minutes before removing to wire rack.

COOKIES

Applesauce Cookies

½ cup shortening
1 cup sugar
1 egg
1 cup applesauce
1¾ cups all-purpose flour
1 tsp. baking soda
½ tsp. salt
1 tsp. cinnamon
½ tsp. nutmeg
½ tsp. cloves
1 cup raisins
1 cup bran flakes cereal

Preheat oven to 375°. In a large bowl, cream shortening and sugar. Beat in egg and applesauce. In a separate bowl, sift together flour, baking soda, salt, cinnamon, nutmeg, and cloves. Stir dry ingredients into wet. Gently fold in raisins and bran flakes. Drop by the tablespoonful onto lightly greased cookie sheets and bake 15 to 17 minutes. Let cool on cookie sheet 5 minutes before removing to wire rack.

Brown Sugar
Freezer Cookies

½ cup butter
1 cup brown sugar
1 egg
2 tsp. vanilla
2 cups all-purpose flour
2 tsp. baking powder
½ tsp. salt
1 cup chopped pecans

In a large bowl, cream butter and brown sugar. Beat in egg and vanilla. In a separate bowl, combine flour, baking

COOKIES

powder, and salt. Stir flour mixture into creamed mixture. Fold in pecans until just combined. With floured hands, roll dough into log and wrap in wax paper. Refrigerate at least 1 hour or up to 24 hours, or freeze up to 3 weeks.

Preheat oven to 350°. Unwrap dough and slice into ½-inch rounds. Arrange rounds on greased baking sheet and bake 10 to 12 minutes until edges are golden. Let cool on cookie sheet 5 minutes before removing to wire rack.

Caramel Chocolate Cookies

1 cup butter, softened
1 cup sugar
1 cup brown sugar
2 eggs
1 T. vanilla
2½ cups all-purpose flour
½ tsp. salt
1 tsp. baking soda
¾ cup cocoa powder
4 dozen caramel candies

In a large bowl, cream butter, sugar, and brown sugar. Beat in eggs and vanilla. Set aside. In a separate bowl, combine flour, salt, baking soda, and cocoa powder. Stir dry ingredients into wet. Cover and chill in refrigerator 2 hours.

Preheat oven to 375°. Work 1 tablespoon of dough around each caramel and roll into ball. Place 2 inches apart on greased cookie sheets and bake 8 minutes. Let cool on cookie sheet 5 minutes before removing to wire rack.

Chocolate Cookies

1 cup butter, softened
1 cup sugar
1 cup brown sugar
2 eggs
2 tsp. vanilla
2 cups all-purpose flour
½ cup cocoa powder
1 tsp. baking soda
½ tsp. salt

Preheat oven to 350°. Cream butter, sugar, and brown sugar in a large bowl. Beat in eggs and vanilla until fluffy. Set aside. In a separate bowl, combine flour, cocoa powder, baking soda, and salt. Stir dry ingredients into wet and mix until just incorporated. Drop by rounded teaspoonfuls onto ungreased cookie sheets. Bake 10 to 12 minutes or until edges are set. Let cool on cookie sheet 5 minutes before removing to wire rack.

Chocolate Chip Cookies

1 cup butter, melted
2 cups brown sugar
6 T. sugar
2 eggs
1 tsp. vanilla
3½ cups all-purpose flour
1 tsp. baking powder
1 tsp. baking soda
1 tsp. salt
2 cups semi-sweet chocolate chips
½ cup chopped walnuts (optional)

Preheat oven to 375°. Cream butter and sugars until light golden. Beat in eggs and vanilla. Set aside. In a separate bowl, combine flour, baking powder, baking soda, and salt. Beat dry ingredients into wet mixture. Stir in chocolate chips and walnuts if desired.

Drop by the tablespoonful onto lightly greased cookie sheets. Bake 8 to 10 minutes. Cookies should look slightly underdone. Let cool on cookie sheet 5 minutes before removing to wire rack.

Chocolate Crinkle Cookies

½ cup shortening
1⅔ cups sugar
2 tsp. vanilla
2 eggs
2 squares unsweetened chocolate, melted
2 cups all-purpose flour, sifted
2 tsp. baking powder
½ tsp. salt
⅓ cup milk
powdered sugar

Thoroughly cream together shortening, sugar, and vanilla. Beat in eggs and then chocolate. Sift dry ingredients together and then add to creamed mixture alternately with milk, blending well after each addition. Chill dough for 2 to 3 hours.

Form into 1-inch balls. Roll in powdered sugar. Place 2 to 3 inches apart on greased cookie sheet. Bake in a preheated 350° oven about 15 minutes.

Cranberry Shortbread Cookies

1 cup butter
¾ cup powdered sugar

1 T. vanilla
1 tsp. almond extract
1 T. grated orange zest
2 cups all-purpose flour
¼ tsp. baking powder
¼ tsp. salt
2 cups sweetened dried cranberries
½ cup chopped pecans

In a large bowl, cream butter and powdered sugar. Stir in vanilla, almond extract, and orange zest. In a separate bowl, combine flour, baking powder, and salt. Stir dry ingredients into creamed mixture. Gently fold in dried cranberries and pecans. Divide dough into 2 portions and roll each half into a 7-inch log. Wrap each log in wax paper and refrigerate at least 4 hours or up to 24 hours.

Preheat oven to 350°. Remove wax paper and slice each log into ½-inch rounds. Arrange rounds on lightly greased baking sheets about 1 inch apart. Bake until firm but not yet brown, 8 to 10 minutes. Let cool on cookie sheet 5 minutes before removing to wire rack.

Cream Cheese Snowballs

½ cup shortening
½ cup butter
½ cup cream cheese
½ cup sugar
½ tsp. vanilla
½ tsp. almond extract
1½ cups all-purpose flour
1 cup powdered sugar
½ cup chopped walnuts

Preheat oven to 350°. In a large bowl, cream shortening, butter, cream cheese, and sugar. Stir in vanilla and almond extract. Stir in flour until combined. Roll into 1-inch balls and place on ungreased cookie sheets about 2

COOKIES

inches apart. Bake until just turning golden, 5 to 7 minutes. While baking, stir together powdered sugar and chopped walnuts. When cookies are done, let stand 2 minutes and then roll in powdered sugar-walnut mixture.

- -

Date and Walnut Drops

½ cup butter
½ cup shortening
1 cup brown sugar
2 eggs
2 T. milk
1½ cups all-purpose flour
¼ tsp. baking soda
¼ tsp. salt
½ tsp. baking powder
1 tsp. cinnamon
½ tsp. cloves
½ tsp. allspice
1 cup chopped dates
1 cup chopped walnuts

Preheat oven to 375°. In a large bowl, cream butter, shortening, and brown sugar. Beat in eggs and milk. In a separate bowl, combine flour, baking soda, salt, baking powder, cinnamon, cloves, and allspice. Stir dry ingredients into creamed mixture. Gently fold in dates and walnuts. Drop by the teaspoonful onto greased cookie sheets, leaving about 2 inches of space between each cookie. Bake 12 to 14 minutes. Let cool on cookie sheet 5 minutes before removing to wire rack.

- -

Gingersnaps

¾ cup shortening
1 cup sugar (plus extra for rolling)

1 egg
¼ cup molasses
2 cups all-purpose flour
2 tsp. baking soda
½ tsp. salt
1 T. ginger
1 tsp. cinnamon

Preheat oven to 350°. Cream shortening and sugar together in a large bowl. Add the egg and beat until light and fluffy. Stir in molasses. In a separate bowl, combine flour, baking soda, salt, ginger, and cinnamon. Fold dry ingredients into creamed mixture and beat until smooth. Shape into small balls and roll in extra sugar. Place 2 inches apart on greased cookie sheets and bake 10 to 12 minutes. Let cool on cookie sheet 5 minutes before removing to wire rack.

- -

Grasshopper Cookies

1 cup butter
⅔ cup sugar
⅔ cup brown sugar
2 eggs
2 tsp. vanilla
2¼ cups all-purpose flour
¾ cup unsweetened cocoa powder
1 tsp. baking soda
1 tsp. salt
1½ cups chocolate or mint chips

Frosting
2 T. butter, softened
3 cups powdered sugar
2 T. milk
3 T. crème de menthe syrup

Preheat oven to 350°. In a large bowl, cream butter, sugar, and brown sugar. Beat in eggs and vanilla. In a separate bowl, combine flour, cocoa powder, baking soda, and salt. Stir dry ingredients into creamed mixture. Fold in chocolate or mint chips. Drop by the rounded teaspoonful onto ungreased cookie sheets. Bake 8 to 10 minutes. Let cool.

To make frosting, cream butter and powdered sugar in bowl. Add milk and crème de menthe syrup and stir until combined. When cookies are cool, dip them into the bowl of frosting to frost halfway up the cookie. Let set on wax paper until frosting hardens.

Jam-Filled Butter Cookies

1½ cups butter, softened
1 cup sugar
3 egg yolks
2¼ tsp. vanilla
⅛ tsp. almond extract
3½ cups all-purpose flour
¼ tsp. salt
½ cup red currant jam
½ cup slivered almonds

Preheat oven to 375°. Cream butter and sugar in a large bowl until light and fluffy. Beat in egg yolks, vanilla, and almond extract. Add flour and salt and stir until combined. Roll into 1-inch balls and place on greased cookie sheets. Using thumb, make a deep indentation in each ball. Bake 7 minutes.

Remove cookies from oven and fill indentations with jam, scattering almonds over top. Return to oven and bake 5 minutes longer. Let cool completely before serving.

COOKIES

Lemon Pudding Cookies

½ cup shortening
½ cup sugar
1 3.75-oz package instant lemon pudding mix
2 eggs
1½ cups all-purpose flour
½ tsp. baking soda
½ tsp. salt

Preheat oven to 375°. In a large bowl, cream shortening, sugar, and pudding mix. Beat in eggs. Blend in flour, baking soda, and salt. Drop by the teaspoonful onto ungreased cookie sheet. Bake 10 to 12 minutes or until just beginning to brown. Let cool on cookie sheet 5 minutes before removing to wire rack.

M&M Cookies

1 cup butter
1 cup sugar
1 cup brown sugar
2 eggs
2 tsp. vanilla
2½ cups all-purpose flour
1 tsp. baking soda
½ tsp. salt
2 cups M&Ms

Preheat oven to 350°. Cream butter, sugar, and brown sugar in a large bowl. Mix in eggs and vanilla. Set aside. In a separate bowl, combine flour, baking soda, and salt. Stir dry ingredients into wet. Blend well and fold in M&Ms. Chill dough in refrigerator 15 minutes. Drop by the tablespoonful onto greased cookie sheet and bake 8 to 10 minutes. Let cool on cookie sheet 5 minutes before removing to wire rack.

COOKIES

Maple Cookies

½ cup butter
1 cup brown sugar
1 egg
½ cup real maple syrup
½ tsp. vanilla
1½ cups all-purpose flour
2 tsp. baking soda
½ tsp. salt
1 cup chopped walnuts

Glaze
2 T. butter, softened
2 T. milk
1 T. real maple syrup
2 cups powdered sugar

Preheat oven to 375°. In a large mixing bowl, cream butter and brown sugar until fluffy. Beat in egg, maple syrup, and vanilla. Set aside. In a separate bowl, combine flour, baking soda, and salt. Stir dry ingredients into wet. Fold in chopped walnuts. Drop by the tablespoonful onto greased cookie sheets and bake 10 to 12 minutes. Let cool completely before preparing glaze.

To make glaze, mix together butter, milk, and maple syrup. Stir in powdered sugar gradually, beating until no lumps remain. Spread over cooled cookies.

Marshmallow-Peanut Crisps

1 lb. white chocolate chips
½ cup peanut butter
1 cup dry roasted peanuts
1½ cups mini marshmallows
1½ cups Rice Krispies cereal

Melt white chocolate chips in a large saucepan over low heat, stirring constantly. Remove from heat and stir in peanut butter. Gently fold in peanuts, marshmallows, and Rice Krispies. Spoon by the rounded tablespoonful onto wax paper and let cool.

Molasses Crinkles

¾ cup butter
1 cup brown sugar
1 egg
¼ cup molasses
2¼ cups all-purpose flour
2 tsp. baking soda
1 tsp. cinnamon
1 tsp. ginger
½ tsp. cloves
¼ tsp. salt
sugar (for rolling)

In a large bowl, cream butter and brown sugar until light and fluffy. Add egg and molasses. Mix well. Add flour, baking soda, cinnamon, ginger, cloves, and salt into creamed mixture and beat until combined. Chill in refrigerator at least 1 hour.

Preheat oven to 375°. Shape rounded tablespoonful of dough into balls and roll in sugar. Place on greased cookie sheets and bake 10 to 12 minutes. Let cool on cookie sheet 5 minutes before removing to wire rack.

COOKIES

Monster Cookies

2 cups butter, softened
4½ cups brown sugar
4 cups white sugar
6½ cups peanut butter
1 dozen eggs
½ cup vanilla
2 T. plus 2 tsp. baking soda
18 cups rolled oats
2¾ cups chocolate chips
2 cups peanuts (or other nuts)
2¾ cups M&Ms

Preheat the oven to 350°. Cream the butter, brown sugar, and white sugar. Add the peanut butter and then mix in the eggs and vanilla. Stir in the baking soda and rolled oats, stirring until well combined. Add the chocolate chips, peanuts, and M&Ms. Drop by the large spoonful onto greased cookie sheets and bake 10 minutes. Let cool on cookie sheet 5 minutes before removing to wire rack.

Oatmeal Cookies

1 cup butter, softened
1 cup packed brown sugar
1 cup white sugar
2 eggs
2 tsp. vanilla
2 cups all-purpose flour
1 tsp. baking soda
½ tsp. salt
1 tsp. cinnamon
3 cups rolled oats
1 cup raisins
1 cup chopped pecans

Preheat the oven to 350°. In a large bowl, cream butter, brown sugar, and white sugar until smooth. Beat in the eggs and vanilla. Set aside. In a separate bowl, combine flour, baking soda, salt, and cinnamon. Stir into creamed mixture. Mix in the oats and then add the raisins and chopped pecans. Drop by the large spoonful onto greased cookie sheets and bake 8 to 10 minutes. Let cool on cookie sheet 5 minutes before removing to wire rack.

As an alternative, try these cookies with chocolate chips, dates, chopped apricots, or walnuts.

Oatmeal Coconut Cookies

1 cup butter
1 cup brown sugar
1 cup sugar
2 eggs
2 tsp. vanilla
2 cups all-purpose flour
1½ tsp. baking powder
¼ tsp. salt
1½ cups rolled oats
1 cup shredded coconut
1 cup semisweet chocolate chips
¾ chopped walnuts

Preheat oven to 350°. In a large bowl, cream butter, brown sugar, and sugar. Stir in eggs and vanilla until fluffy. Set aside. In a separate bowl, combine flour, baking powder, salt, and rolled oats. Stir dry ingredients into wet. Fold in shredded coconut, chocolate chips, and walnuts. Drop by the teaspoonful onto greased cookie sheets. Bake 8 to 10 minutes or until just beginning to brown. Let cool on cookie sheet 5 minutes before removing to wire rack.

COOKIES

Oatmeal Raisin Cookies

1 cup raisins
1 cup water
1 cup shortening
1 cup sugar
2 eggs
1 tsp. vanilla
2 cups all-purpose flour
¾ tsp. baking soda
1 tsp. salt
1½ cups rolled oats

In a small saucepan, cook raisins and water until only 5 tablespoons of liquid remain. Drain raisins, reserving liquid.

Preheat oven to 375°. In a large bowl, mix together shortening, sugar, and eggs. Stir in vanilla and cooled liquid from raisins. Set aside. In a separate bowl, mix together flour, baking soda, and salt. Fold dry ingredients into wet. Stir in oats and cooked raisins.

Drop by the teaspoonful 2 inches apart on lightly greased cookie sheets. Bake 8 minutes until lightly browned. Let cool on cookie sheet 5 minutes before removing to wire rack.

Peanut Butter Cookies

1 cup butter
1¼ cups crunchy peanut butter
1 cup packed brown sugar
1 cup white sugar
2 eggs
1 tsp. vanilla
2¾ cups all-purpose flour
1 tsp. baking powder
½ tsp. salt
1½ tsp. baking soda
additional sugar (for rolling)

In a large bowl, cream together butter, peanut butter, brown sugar, and white sugar until smooth. Beat in eggs and vanilla until blended. In a separate bowl, combine flour, baking powder, salt, and baking soda. Stir into creamed mixture. Cover bowl and refrigerate until firm, at least an hour.

Preheat the oven to 375°. Roll dough into 1-inch balls and roll in additional sugar. Place on greased cookie sheets and flatten with fork, creating crisscross pattern. Bake 7 to 9 minutes. Do not overbake. Cookies should still be soft. Let cool on cookie sheet 5 minutes before removing to wire rack.

Peppermint Sugar Cookies

¾ cup butter-flavored shortening
½ cup brown sugar
½ cup sugar
1 egg
2 T. milk
1 T. vanilla
2 cups all-purpose flour
1 tsp. salt
¾ tsp. baking soda
¾ cup crushed candy canes, divided

Preheat oven to 350°. In a large bowl, cream shortening, brown sugar, and sugar. Beat in egg, milk, and vanilla. In a separate bowl, combine flour, salt, and baking soda. Stir dry ingredients into creamed mixture. Gently fold in ½ cup crushed candy canes and shape into 1-inch balls. Place about 2 inches apart on lightly greased cookie sheet. Bake 8 to 10 minutes. After removing from oven, immediately sprinkle each cookie with a bit of the remaining crushed candy. Let cool on cookie sheet 5 minutes before removing to wire rack.

Pralines

1 cup brown sugar
1 cup sugar
½ cup cream
1½ cups halved pecans
2 T. butter

Combine brown sugar, sugar, and cream in heavy 2-quart saucepan and bring to a boil over medium heat. Cook, stirring occasionally, until mixture forms a thick syrup. Stir in pecans and butter. Continue to cook over medium heat, stirring frequently.

Remove from heat and let cool 10 minutes. Drop by the tablespoonful onto wax paper, leaving 3 inches between. Let cool at least 1 hour before serving.

Pumpkin Cookies

1 cup butter
½ cup sugar
½ cup brown sugar
1 cup pumpkin
1 tsp. vanilla
1 egg
2 cups all-purpose flour
1 tsp. baking soda
1 tsp. baking powder
1 tsp. cinnamon
¼ tsp. salt

Frosting
3 T. butter
½ cup brown sugar
¼ cup milk
1½ cups powdered sugar

Preheat oven to 350°. In a large bowl, cream together butter, sugar, and brown sugar. Stir in pumpkin, vanilla, and egg. Beat until smooth. In a separate bowl, combine flour, baking soda, baking powder, cinnamon, and salt. Fold dry ingredients into pumpkin mixture. Drop by the rounded tablespoonful onto greased cookie sheets and bake 10 to 12 minutes. Let cool on wire rack before frosting.

When cookies have cooled, combine butter and brown sugar in a small saucepan. Bring to a boil, stirring constantly. When mixture has thickened, remove from heat and let cool 10 minutes. Stir in milk and powdered sugar. Frost cookies immediately.

Sand Tarts

1 cup butter, room temperature
2 cups sugar
1 tsp. salt
2 tsp. vanilla
3 eggs, separated
3 cups all-purpose flour

Topping
¼ cup sugar
¾ tsp. cinnamon
1 egg, beaten
4 cups shelled, whole pecans

In a large mixing bowl, beat the butter until smooth. Add the sugar and beat until smooth and creamy. Add the salt and vanilla and blend well. In a small bowl, beat the egg yolks thoroughly and then add to the butter mixture. In a separate bowl, beat the egg whites until stiff peaks form. Use a rubber spatula to gently but thoroughly fold the whites into the butter mixture. (There will still be some spots of egg whites, but that's okay.) Add 1½ cups of the

COOKIES

flour and fold in gently. Then add the remaining 1½ cups flour and fold in gently again. Cover the bowl and chill the dough for at least 8 hours or overnight.

When ready to bake, mix together the sugar and cinnamon in a small bowl. In another small bowl, beat the egg. Divide the dough into quarters and work with one quarter at a time, returning the other quarters to the refrigerator to stay cold until needed. Roll the dough very thin and then cut out cookies using a cookie cutter or a sharp knife. Brush the tops of the cookies with the egg and then sprinkle on a bit of cinnamon sugar. Top each cookie with a whole pecan. Bake in a preheated 350° oven 9 to 10 minutes, watching carefully and adjusting time as necessary so cookies don't get too brown.

Shortbread Cookies

2 cups butter, softened
1 cup sugar
2 tsp. vanilla
4 cups all-purpose flour
½ cup powdered sugar (optional)

Preheat oven to 350°. In a large bowl, cream butter and sugar until light and fluffy. Stir in vanilla. Add flour and mix until well combined. Form dough into 2 logs, each about 2 inches wide. Refrigerate 30 minutes. When chilled, slice into cookies ¼-inch thick and set on greased cookie sheets. Bake 8 to 10 minutes. If desired dust with powdered sugar while still warm.

Snickerdoodles

1½ cups sugar
½ cup butter, softened

1 tsp. vanilla
2 eggs
2¾ cups all-purpose flour
1 tsp. cream of tartar
½ tsp. baking soda
¼ tsp. salt
2 T. sugar
2 tsp. cinnamon

Preheat oven to 400°. In a large bowl, cream 1½ cups sugar and butter until light and fluffy. Mix in vanilla and eggs and set aside. In a separate bowl, combine flour, cream of tartar, baking soda, and salt. Stir dry ingredients into wet.

Combine 2 tablespoons sugar and cinnamon in a small bowl. Shape dough into 1-inch balls and roll in cinnamon sugar. Place on ungreased cookie sheets and bake 8 to 10 minutes or until edges are just beginning to brown. Remove from sheets and let cool on wire racks.

Soft Molasses Cookies

1 cup molasses
1 cup sugar
⅔ cup shortening, melted
1 cup water
5 cups all-purpose flour
1 tsp. ginger
1 tsp. cinnamon
2 tsp. baking soda
1¾ tsp. salt

Preheat oven to 425°. In a large bowl, combine molasses, sugar, melted shortening, and water. In a separate bowl, combine flour, ginger, cinnamon, baking soda, and salt. Fold dry ingredients into wet and blend until smooth.

COOKIES

Drop by the rounded teaspoonful onto greased cookie sheets and bake 10 to 12 minutes. Let cool on cookie sheet 5 minutes before removing to wire rack.

Sugar Cookies

½ cup butter
½ cup shortening
2 cups sugar
2 eggs
1 cup buttermilk
1 T. vanilla
4 cups all-purpose flour
1¼ tsp. salt
1 tsp. baking soda
½ tsp. nutmeg

Preheat oven to 375°. Cream butter, shortening, and sugar in a large bowl. Beat in eggs, buttermilk, and vanilla until combined. Set aside. In a separate bowl, combine flour, salt, baking soda, and nutmeg. Fold dry ingredients into wet a little at a time. Drop by the rounded teaspoonful onto greased cookie sheets and bake 10 minutes. Let cool on cookie sheet 5 minutes before removing to wire rack.

White Chocolate Chip Cookies

1 cup butter
1 cup sugar
¾ cup brown sugar
2 eggs
1 tsp. vanilla
1 cup cocoa powder
1¾ cups all-purpose flour

1½ tsp. baking soda
½ tsp. salt
2 cups white chocolate chips

Preheat oven to 350°. In a large bowl, cream butter, sugar, and brown sugar. Add eggs and vanilla and beat until light and fluffy. Set aside. In a separate bowl, combine cocoa powder, flour, baking soda, and salt. Stir dry ingredients into wet. Fold in white chocolate chips. Drop by the rounded tablespoonful onto greased cookie sheets and bake 8 to 10 minutes, until just set. Let cool on cookie sheet 5 minutes before removing to wire rack.

White Chocolate Macadamia Nut Cookies

½ cup butter
½ cup shortening
½ cup sugar
¾ cup brown sugar
2 eggs
½ tsp. vanilla
½ tsp. almond extract
2½ cups all-purpose flour
1 tsp. baking soda
½ tsp. salt
1 cup chopped macadamia nuts
1 cup white chocolate chips

Preheat oven to 350°. In a large bowl, cream butter, shortening, sugar, and brown sugar until smooth. Beat in eggs, vanilla, and almond extract. In a separate bowl, combine flour, baking soda, and salt. Stir dry ingredients into creamed mixture. Gently fold in chopped nuts and white chocolate chips. Drop by the tablespoonful onto ungreased cookie sheets. Bake 8 to 10 minutes or until golden brown. Let cool on cookie sheet 5 minutes before removing to wire rack.

COOKIES

BARS

For we are unto God a sweet savour of Christ.

2 Corinthians 2:15

That old pan in your cupboard isn't just for casseroles. Break out the pan and indulge in one of these mouth-watering treats. Need a fresh dessert for a summertime picnic? Try a berry crisp with the berries you just picked. Hoping for a healthy treat you can munch on the go? Whip up some granola bars with oatmeal and raisins. Want a chocolatey dessert for a cozy wintertime gathering? You can't go wrong with brownies. Enjoy these delicious recipes—sure to become family favorites!

Almond Bars

1 cup butter
1½ cups almond paste
1¾ cups sugar
2 eggs
2 cups all-purpose flour
½ tsp. salt
½ cup slivered almonds

Preheat oven to 300°. Bring butter and almond paste to room temperature and cream together in a large bowl. Beat in sugar and eggs and then add flour and salt. Stir until well combined. Pour into a greased 9 x 13-inch pan and sprinkle nuts over top. Bake 35 to 40 minutes or until golden. Let cool completely before cutting into bars.

Apple Butter Bars

½ cup butter
½ cup brown sugar
¼ cup sugar
1 egg
1 tsp. vanilla
¾ cup apple butter
1½ cups all-purpose flour
¼ tsp. salt
¼ tsp. baking soda
½ tsp. cinnamon
¼ tsp. nutmeg
1 cup raisins

Glaze
1 cup powdered sugar
¼ tsp. vanilla
2 T. milk

Preheat oven to 350°. In a large bowl, cream butter, brown sugar, and sugar. Mix in egg, vanilla, and apple butter until combined. Set aside. In a separate bowl, combine flour, salt, baking soda, cinnamon, and nutmeg. Stir dry ingredients into wet. Fold in raisins. Spread batter into a greased and floured 9 x 13-inch pan and bake 20 to 25 minutes or until knife inserted into center comes out clean. Let cool completely before preparing glaze.

To make glaze, combine powdered sugar, vanilla, and milk in a small bowl. Drizzle over cooled bars.

Apple Butterscotch Bars

1½ cups all-purpose flour
1½ tsp. baking powder
¾ tsp. salt
1½ cups rolled oats
⅓ cup sugar
⅔ cup brown sugar
1 cup butter, softened
1½ cups apple butter
¼ cup chopped nuts
1 11-oz. package (1⅔ cups) butterscotch chips

Preheat oven to 375°. In a large bowl, stir together flour, baking powder, salt, oats, sugar, and brown sugar. Using a pastry blender, cut butter into oat mixture. Set aside ¾ cup of this mixture. Press remaining mix into bottom of greased 9-inch square pan. Spread apple butter over top and set aside.

Combine chopped nuts, butterscotch chips, and reserved oat mixture in a medium bowl. Sprinkle over apple butter and bake 30 to 35 minutes or until golden. Let cool completely before cutting into bars and serving.

Apricot Date Bars

1½ cups brown sugar, divided
1 cup chopped dates
1½ cups dried apricots, chopped
½ cup orange juice
¾ cup butter, melted
1 tsp. vanilla
2 cups all-purpose flour
1 tsp. baking soda
½ tsp. salt
2 cups rolled oats

Preheat oven to 350°. Combine ½ cup brown sugar, dates, apricots, and orange juice in a saucepan. Bring to a simmer over medium heat and cook, stirring frequently, about 5 minutes or until mixture has thickened. Set aside and let cool.

Mix together melted butter, vanilla, and remaining 1 cup brown sugar. Set aside. In a separate bowl, mix together flour, baking soda, salt, and rolled oats. Stir dry ingredients into wet mixture and mix until combined. Press half of this mixture into bottom of greased 9 x 13-inch pan. Spread cooled apricot-date mixture evenly over crust. Crumble remaining oat mixture over top. Bake about 30 minutes or until top is golden brown. Let cool completely before cutting into bars and serving.

Banana Date Bars

½ cup butter
1 cup sugar
2 eggs
1 tsp. vanilla
2 cups all-purpose flour
1 tsp. baking powder
½ tsp. baking soda

¼ tsp. salt
2 cups sliced bananas
1 cup dates, pitted and chopped
½ cup chopped walnuts

Preheat oven to 350°. In a large bowl, cream butter and sugar. Whisk in eggs and vanilla until well combined. Set aside. In a separate bowl, combine flour, baking powder, baking soda, and salt. Stir dry ingredients into wet and mix well. Using rubber spatula, gradually fold in sliced bananas, dates, and walnuts. Spread batter evenly into a greased 9 x 13-inch baking pan. Bake 30 to 35 minutes. Let cool completely before cutting into squares.

- -

Blondies

⅔ cup butter, melted
2 cups brown sugar
2 eggs, lightly beaten
2 tsp. vanilla
2 cups all-purpose flour
1 tsp. baking powder
¼ tsp. baking soda
1 tsp. salt
1 cup chopped walnuts
2 cups semisweet chocolate chips

Preheat oven to 350°. In a large bowl, mix melted butter and brown sugar until well blended. Add beaten eggs and vanilla. Set aside. In a separate bowl, combine flour, baking powder, baking soda, and salt. Add dry ingredients to wet mixture. Fold in walnuts and chocolate chips. Pour batter into a greased 9 x 13-inch pan and bake 20 to 25 minutes. Do not overbake.

BARS

Blueberry Shortbread Bars

1½ cups all-purpose flour
½ cup sugar
½ tsp. salt
¼ tsp. baking powder
¼ tsp. nutmeg
½ cup cold butter, cubed
1 egg yolk
1 tsp. ice water
1 cup fresh blueberries

Preheat oven to 375°. In a large bowl, whisk together flour, sugar, salt, baking powder, and nutmeg. Using a pastry blender, cut in cold butter until mixture resembles coarse crumbs. Mix in egg yolk and ice water and continue blending until well combined.

Press ¾ of the mixture into the bottom of an ungreased 9-inch square baking dish. Scatter the blueberries over the crust. Crumble the remaining dough over the blueberries and bake until golden, 30 to 35 minutes. Let cool completely before cutting into bars.

Brownies

3 1-oz. squares unsweetened chocolate
1 cup butter
2 cups sugar
¼ tsp. salt
1 T. vanilla
4 eggs
1 cup all-purpose flour
1 cup chopped walnuts

Preheat oven to 350°. In a medium saucepan, melt chocolate squares and butter over low heat, stirring constantly. Pour into large bowl and stir in sugar, salt, and vanilla.

Beat until well blended. Whisk in eggs. Stir in flour until just combined. Fold in chopped walnuts. Pour mixture into a greased 9 x 13-inch pan and bake 35 minutes.

-- --

Caramel Bars

32 caramel candies
5 T. heavy cream
2 cups all-purpose flour
2 cups rolled oats
1½ cups brown sugar
1 tsp. baking soda
½ tsp. salt
1 cup butter, melted
½ cup milk
½ cup semisweet chocolate chips
½ cup chopped walnuts

Preheat oven to 350°. Melt caramels and heavy cream in a saucepan over low heat, stirring occasionally, until smooth. Set aside. In a large bowl, combine the flour, rolled oats, brown sugar, baking soda, and salt. Add the melted butter and milk and stir until combined. Press half the oat mixture into a greased 9 x 13-inch baking pan, setting the remainder aside.

Bake crust 8 minutes. Remove from oven and sprinkle with chocolate chips and walnuts. Pour reserved caramel mixture over chocolate chips and walnuts. Crumble remaining oat mixture over caramel. Return to oven and bake 15 minutes longer or until crust turns golden brown. Let cool slightly before cutting into squares. Serve warm.

BARS

Cheesecake Bars

Crust
⅓ cup butter, softened
⅓ cup brown sugar
⅓ cup chopped walnuts
1 cup all-purpose flour

Filling
¼ cup sugar
2 8-oz. packages cream cheese
2 T. lemon juice
¼ cup milk
2 eggs
1 tsp. vanilla

Topping
¼ cup seedless raspberry jam
½ cup chocolate chips

Preheat oven to 350°. To make crust, cream butter and brown sugar until fluffy. Stir in chopped walnuts and flour. Combine until mixture becomes crumbles. Press into bottom of a 9-inch square baking pan. Bake 12 to 15 minutes.

Meanwhile, prepare filling. In a large bowl, cream sugar and cream cheese. Beat in lemon juice, milk, eggs, and vanilla. Spread filling over baked crust and bake 25 to 30 minutes. Let cool 20 minutes.

To make topping, melt raspberry jam and chocolate chips separately. Drizzle each over top of filling. Refrigerate until ready to serve.

Cheesecake Blondies

Blondie Layer
1 cup shortening
1 cup brown sugar
½ cup sugar
2 tsp. vanilla
3 eggs
2 cups all-purpose flour
1 tsp. baking soda
½ tsp. salt
1½ cups semisweet chocolate chips

Cheesecake layer
2 8-oz. packages cream cheese
¼ cup sugar
2 eggs
1 cup chopped walnuts

Preheat oven to 350°. To make blondie layer, cream shortening, brown sugar, and sugar. Beat in vanilla and eggs until smooth. Set aside. In a separate bowl, combine flour, baking soda, and salt. Stir dry ingredients into wet until just combined. Fold in chocolate chips and set aside.

To make cheesecake layer, mix together cream cheese and sugar in a separate bowl. Beat in eggs.

Spread half of blondie dough in the bottom of a greased 9 x 13-inch pan. Pour cream cheese mixture over dough and sprinkle with chopped walnuts. Drop pieces of remaining dough over cream cheese layer. Bake 45 minutes or until golden. Let cool completely before cutting into bars.

BARS

Cherry Pie Bars

1 cup butter, softened
1¾ cups sugar
4 eggs
1 tsp. vanilla
1 tsp. almond extract
2½ cups all-purpose flour
1½ tsp. baking powder
½ tsp. salt
1 21-oz can cherry pie filling

Glaze
½ cup powdered sugar
3 T. milk
¼ cup slivered almonds

Preheat oven to 350°. In a large bowl, cream the butter and sugar until light and fluffy. Beat in the eggs, vanilla, and almond extract. Set aside. In a separate bowl, combine the flour, baking powder, and salt. Stir dry ingredients into wet mixture. Reserve 1½ cups of batter. Pour remaining batter into a greased jelly roll pan. Cover with cherry pie filling. Drop reserved batter by the spoonful over cherry layer. Bake 40 minutes or until top is golden. Let cool.

To make glaze, mix powdered sugar and milk in a small bowl and drizzle over top of bars. Sprinkle slivered almonds over top.

Chewy Granola Bars

3 cups instant oats
1 14-oz. can sweetened condensed milk
2 T. butter, melted
1 cup shredded coconut
1 cup sliced almonds

BARS

1 cup dried cherries
1 cup semisweet chocolate chips

Preheat oven to 350°. In a large bowl, mix together the oats, sweetened condensed milk, melted butter, coconut, almonds, dried cherries, and chocolate chips. Press into a greased 9 x 13-inch pan. Bake 20 minutes until just browned around the edges. Immediately cut into squares and let cool completely before serving.

Note: Any combination of fruits and sweets can be used in these granola bars. Try dried cranberries, pecans, walnuts, M&Ms, peanuts, raisins, and chopped dried apricots!

Chocolate Orange Bars

½ cup butter, softened
1¼ cups brown sugar, divided
2 eggs, separated
2 T. grated orange zest
⅓ cup orange juice
1¼ cups all-purpose flour
1 tsp. baking powder
¼ tsp. salt
½ cup chocolate chips
¼ cup chopped walnuts

Preheat oven to 325°. In a large bowl, cream the butter and ½ cup brown sugar until combined. Beat in egg yolks, orange zest, and orange juice. In a separate bowl, combine flour, baking powder, and salt. Stir dry ingredients into wet. Pour batter into a greased 9 x 13-inch pan and sprinkle with chocolate chips and walnuts.

Beat the egg whites and remaining ¾ cup brown sugar until stiff and glossy. Dollop over batter and spread until even. Bake until meringue begins to turn golden, about 35 minutes. Let cool before cutting into squares.

Chocolate Peanut Butter Bars

1 cup butter, melted
¼ cup sugar
⅔ cup brown sugar
½ tsp. salt
3 cups rolled oats
¾ cup chocolate chips
¾ cup peanut butter

Preheat oven to 350°. In a large bowl, combine melted butter, sugar, brown sugar, and salt. Stir in oats and press into a 9 x 13-inch pan. Bake 15 minutes. Let cool.

Melt chocolate chips and peanut butter together in a saucepan over low heat, stirring constantly. Spread over baked crust and refrigerate until firm, about 1 hour.

Cinnamon Bars

1 cup butter, softened
1 cup sugar
1 egg
1 tsp. vanilla
2 cups all-purpose flour
1½ T. cinnamon
1 tsp. baking soda
1 tsp. salt
1½ cups chopped walnuts

Frosting
1 8-oz. package cream cheese
½ cup butter
2 cups powdered sugar
2 tsp. vanilla
1 to 2 T. milk

BARS

Preheat oven to 325°. In a large bowl, cream butter and sugar. Beat in egg and vanilla and set aside. In a separate bowl, combine flour, cinnamon, baking soda, and salt. Stir dry ingredients into wet. Fold in chopped walnuts and spread batter evenly in a greased 9 x 13-inch pan. Bake 22 to 25 minutes or until golden brown. Let cool completely before frosting.

To make frosting, blend cream cheese and butter together. Mix in powdered sugar, vanilla, and milk to desired consistency. Spread over bars.

Cinnamon Coffee Bars

¼ cup butter, softened
1 cup brown sugar
1 egg plus 1 yolk
¾ cup hot coffee
1½ cups all-purpose flour
¼ tsp. salt
1 tsp. baking powder
¼ tsp. baking soda
1 T. cinnamon
½ cup raisins
¼ cup chopped nuts

Preheat oven to 350°. In a large bowl, cream butter and brown sugar. Beat in egg and yolk. Carefully whisk in hot coffee until combined. Set aside. In a separate bowl, mix together flour, salt, baking powder, baking soda, and cinnamon. Stir dry ingredients into coffee mixture. Fold in raisins and chopped nuts. Pour batter into a greased 9 x 13-inch baking pan. Bake 18 to 20 minutes or until knife inserted into center comes out clean. Let cool completely before cutting into bars and serving.

BARS

Coconut Bars

First Layer
½ cup butter
¼ cup sugar
3 T. cocoa powder
1 egg, beaten
1 tsp. vanilla
2 cups graham cracker crumbs
1 cup coconut flakes
½ cup chopped nuts (optional)

Second Layer
¼ cup butter, softened
2 cups powdered sugar
2 T. instant vanilla pudding mix
2 T. hot water

Third Layer
½ cup semisweet chocolate chips
1 T. butter

To make first layer, combine butter, sugar, and cocoa powder in top of double boiler. Boil water in bottom. Cook, stirring frequently, until butter melts and sugar dissolves. Add beaten egg and vanilla. Cook, stirring constantly, 3 minutes longer. Remove from heat. Using a rubber spatula, fold in graham cracker crumbs, coconut flakes, and nuts (optional). Pat mixture into the bottom of an 8-inch square pan. Place in refrigerator to chill.

Prepare second layer while first layer chills. Cream butter, powdered sugar, and vanilla pudding mix. Blend in hot water. Mix well and then spread over first layer. Return pan to refrigerator to continue chilling.

For third layer, melt chocolate chips and butter in top of double boiler, stirring constantly. Drizzle over second layer. Refrigerate until chocolate is firm. Cut into squares to serve. This recipe freezes well.

Cranberry Bars

4 cups cranberries
1⅓ cups sugar
3 T. orange zest
½ cup orange juice
1 cup unsweetened applesauce
1½ cups all-purpose flour
2 cups rolled oats
1 cup brown sugar
1 tsp. salt
1 tsp. cinnamon
1 cup butter
½ cup chopped walnuts

Preheat oven to 350°. Combine cranberries, sugar, orange zest, and orange juice in a saucepan over medium heat. Bring to a boil and then reduce heat to simmer. Cook, stirring frequently, until mixture has reduced to about 2 cups. Remove from heat and stir in applesauce. Set aside to cool.

In medium bowl, combine flour, oats, brown sugar, salt, and cinnamon. Cut in the butter using a pastry blender until the mixture resembles coarse crumbs. Add walnuts. Press half this mixture into a greased 9 x 13-inch baking pan and spread the cranberry sauce over top. Crumble the remaining oat mixture over filling. Bake 25 minutes or until top is golden brown. Let cool completely before cutting into bars.

BARS

Crispy Chocolate Crackles

¼ cup cocoa powder
3 T. butter
¼ cup corn syrup
¼ cup brown sugar
3 cups Rice Krispies
1 cup mini marshmallows

Combine cocoa powder, butter, corn syrup, and brown sugar in a large saucepan. Cook over medium-low heat, stirring constantly, until mixture comes to a boil. Remove from heat and gently fold in the Rice Krispies and marshmallows. Spread into a buttered 9-inch square pan and pat down. Let cool completely before cutting into squares.

Date Nut Squares

⅓ cup boiling water
2 cups dates, pitted and chopped
½ cup shortening
1 cup sugar
2 eggs
1 cup all-purpose flour
¾ tsp. salt
¼ tsp. baking soda
½ tsp. cinnamon
½ tsp. nutmeg
¾ cup chopped walnuts

Preheat oven to 325°. Pour boiling water over dates and set aside to cool. In large bowl, cream together the shortening and sugar. Add eggs and beat well. In a separate bowl, combine the flour, salt, baking soda, cinnamon, and nutmeg. Stir dry ingredients into wet and mix well. Fold in the chopped walnuts and dates along with any liquid. Spread mixture evenly in greased 9-inch square pan. Bake 45 minutes and let cool completely before serving.

Dream Bars

First Layer
½ cup butter
½ cup brown sugar
1 cup all-purpose flour

Second Layer
2 T. all-purpose flour
1 cup brown sugar
¼ tsp. salt
½ tsp. baking powder
2 eggs, beaten
1 tsp. vanilla
1½ cups shredded coconut
1 cup chopped nuts

Preheat oven to 350°. To make first layer, cream butter and brown sugar together in a medium bowl. Blend in flour and mix until crumbly. Pat into 9-inch square pan and bake 15 minutes.

To make second layer, mix flour, brown sugar, salt, and baking powder in a large bowl. Stir in beaten eggs and vanilla. Fold in shredded coconut and chopped nuts. Pour mixture over crust and bake 20 to 25 minutes longer. Let cool before cutting into squares.

Gooey Nut Squares

½ cup butter
¾ cup brown sugar, divided
1¼ cups plus 3 T. all-purpose flour
1 tsp. baking powder
1 cup chopped nuts, divided
2 eggs
¾ cup corn syrup
½ tsp. salt
1 tsp. vanilla

Preheat oven to 350°. Cream butter and ½ cup brown sugar in a large bowl. Add 1¼ cups flour and baking powder. Fold in ¼ cup chopped nuts. Pat firmly into 9 x 13-inch pan and bake 7 minutes. Remove from oven.

In clean bowl, beat eggs until foamy. Stir in corn syrup, remaining ¼ cup brown sugar, salt, and vanilla until combined. Stir in remaining 3 T. flour. Spread mixture over baked crust. Sprinkle remaining ¾ cup nuts over topping and bake 12 to 15 minutes longer. Let cool 10 minutes before cutting into squares.

Granola Bars

2 cups rolled oats
¾ cup brown sugar
½ cup wheat germ
¾ tsp. cinnamon
1 cup flour
¾ tsp. salt
¾ cup raisins
½ cup honey
1 egg, beaten
½ cup vegetable oil
2 tsp. vanilla

Preheat oven to 350°. In a large bowl, mix together the oats, brown sugar, wheat germ, cinnamon, flour, salt, and raisins. Make a well in the center and mix in honey, beaten egg, vegetable oil, and vanilla. Mix until thoroughly combined. Pat into a greased 9 x 13-inch pan and bake 30 to 35 minutes. Cut into bars immediately and let cool before serving.

Lemon Bars

First Layer
2 cups all-purpose flour
1 cup butter
½ cup powdered sugar

Second Layer
2 cups sugar
¼ cup all-purpose flour
¼ tsp. salt
4 eggs, beaten
¼ cup lemon juice
¼ cup powdered sugar

Preheat oven to 350°. To make first layer, cream flour, butter, and powdered sugar together and press dough into a greased 9 x 13-inch pan. Bake 20 minutes.

While crust is baking, prepare second layer. Combine sugar, flour, and salt in a large bowl. Stir in beaten eggs and lemon juice. Whisk until well combined. Pour over crust and return pan to oven, baking 25 minutes longer. Dust with powdered sugar while still warm.

BARS

Lemon Blondies

½ cup butter
¾ cup sugar
2 eggs
2 T. lemon juice
1 T. lemon zest
1 tsp. vanilla
¾ cup all-purpose flour
¼ tsp. salt

Glaze
1 cup powdered sugar
3 T. lemon juice
1 tsp. lemon zest

Preheat oven to 350°. Cream butter and sugar in a large bowl. Beat in eggs, lemon juice, lemon zest, and vanilla. Stir in flour and salt. Beat until well combined. Pour batter into a greased 8-inch square pan. Bake 23 to 25 minutes. Let cool completely before preparing glaze.

To make glaze, mix together powdered sugar, lemon juice, and lemon zest. Drizzle over cooled bars and cut into squares.

Lemon Cheesecake Bars

Crust
1½ cups all-purpose flour
½ cup powdered sugar
¾ cup butter, cubed

Lemon Layer
4 eggs
1½ cups sugar
1 T. all-purpose flour
2 T. lemon zest
½ cup lemon juice

Cream Layer
2 8-oz. packages cream cheese
1 cup sugar
2 eggs, beaten

Preheat oven to 350°. To make crust, whisk together flour and powdered sugar in a medium bowl. Using a pastry blender, cut in butter cubes until mixture resembles coarse crumbs. Press mixture into the bottom and up the sides of a greased 9 x 13-inch pan. Bake 15 minutes or until golden.

To make lemon layer, whisk together eggs and sugar until smooth. Stir in flour, lemon zest, and lemon juice. Pour mixture into crust and set aside.

To make cream layer, beat cream cheese and sugar until smooth. Beat in eggs. Spread over lemon layer in pan. (Mixtures will separate during baking.) Bake 30 minutes or until filling is set. Let cool completely before serving.

Peanut Butter Oatmeal Bars

2 cups quick-cooking oats
1 cup all-purpose flour
1 cup brown sugar
½ tsp. salt
½ tsp. baking soda
¾ cup butter, softened
1 14-oz. can sweetened condensed milk
¾ cup peanut butter

Preheat oven to 350°. In a large bowl, combine oats, flour, brown sugar, salt, and baking soda. Using a pastry blender, cut in butter until mixture is crumbly. Reserve 1½ cups of mixture and set aside. Pat the remaining oat mixture into the bottom of a greased 9 x 13-inch pan. Set aside. In a medium bowl, stir together the sweetened condensed milk and peanut butter. Spread evenly over

BARS

181

crust. Crumble reserved oat mixture over filling and bake 30 to 35 minutes or until golden. Let cool completely before cutting into squares.

Peanut Butter Brownies

Brownies
2 1-oz. squares unsweetened chocolate
½ cup butter
2 eggs
1 cup sugar
½ cup all-purpose flour

Filling
½ cup creamy peanut butter
¼ cup butter, softened
1½ cups powdered sugar
2 to 3 T. milk

Glaze
1 1-oz. square unsweetened chocolate
1 T. butter

To make brownies, preheat oven to 350°. In a small saucepan, melt chocolate and butter over low heat. Pour into large bowl. Beat in eggs, sugar, and flour. Pour batter into a greased 9-inch square pan and bake 25 minutes. Let cool.

To make filling, cream peanut butter, butter, and powdered sugar in a medium bowl. Add milk to desired consistency. Spread filling over brownies.

To make glaze, melt chocolate and butter over low heat in a small saucepan. Drizzle over filling. Chill until ready to serve. Store in refrigerator.

Peanut Butter Crispies

¼ cup butter
¾ cup peanut butter
4 cups miniature marshmallows
5 cups crisp rice cereal

Melt butter in a large saucepan over low heat. Stir in peanut butter until combined. Add in marshmallows and stir until melted. Remove from heat and add cereal. Stir until well coated and then press mixture into a greased 9 x 13-inch pan. Let cool before cutting into squares.

Pumpkin Bars

1¼ cups all-purpose flour
¼ tsp. salt
1 tsp. pumpkin pie spice
½ tsp. baking powder
½ tsp. baking soda
2 eggs
¼ cup vegetable oil
1 cup sugar
2 cups pumpkin
¾ cup raisins
½ cup walnuts

Glaze
½ cup powdered sugar
1 T. maple syrup

Preheat oven to 350°. In a medium bowl, combine flour, salt, pumpkin pie spice, baking powder, and baking soda. Set aside. In a separate bowl, beat together the eggs, vegetable oil, and sugar until smooth. Beat in the pumpkin. Stir dry ingredients into pumpkin mixture and beat until well combined. Fold in raisins and walnuts. Pour mixture into a greased and floured 9 x 13-inch baking pan.

BARS

Bake 30 to 40 minutes or until knife inserted into center comes out clean. Let cool completely before preparing glaze.

To make glaze, combine powdered sugar and maple syrup. Drizzle over cooled bars.

Pumpkin Ice Cream Bars

First Layer
16 graham crackers, crushed
¼ cup brown sugar
¼ cup butter, melted
1 qt. softened vanilla ice cream

Second Layer
1 cup pumpkin
¾ cup sugar
½ tsp. salt
¼ cup brown sugar
¼ tsp. ginger
¼ tsp. cloves
½ tsp. cinnamon
2 cups heavy cream

To make first layer, combine graham cracker crumbs, brown sugar, and melted butter in a large bowl. Press into bottom of 9 x 13-inch pan. Spread softened ice cream over top. Freeze until firm.

Meanwhile, make second layer by combining pumpkin, sugar, salt, brown sugar, ginger, cloves, and cinnamon in a large bowl. Set aside. In a separate bowl, whip cream until soft peaks form. Fold whipped cream into pumpkin mixture. Spread over ice cream and freeze until firm.

S'mores Bars

½ cup butter, softened
¾ cup sugar
1 egg
½ cup all-purpose flour
1 cup graham cracker crumbs
1 tsp. baking powder
¼ tsp. salt
1½ cups milk chocolate chips
3 cups miniature marshmallows

Preheat oven to 350°. In a large bowl, cream butter and sugar. Mix in egg until fluffy. Beat in flour, graham cracker crumbs, baking powder, and salt until combined. Spread batter into a greased 9 x 13-inch baking dish. Bake 10 minutes or until just set. Sprinkle chocolate chips and marshmallows over top and bake 10 to 12 minutes longer or until marshmallows are lightly browned. Let cool completely before cutting into bars.

Zucchini Nut Squares

1 cup honey
¼ cup butter, melted
3 eggs
1¼ cups all-purpose flour
¼ tsp. salt
1 tsp. baking powder
¾ cup grated zucchini
1 cup chopped walnuts
1 cup dates, pitted and chopped
⅓ cup powdered sugar

Preheat oven to 350°. In a large bowl, whisk together honey, melted butter, and eggs. Beat well and set aside. In a separate bowl, combine flour, salt, and baking powder. Stir dry ingredients into egg mixture. Fold in zucchini,

BARS

walnuts, and dates. Spread mixture into a greased 9 x 13-inch baking pan and bake 25 to 30 minutes or until golden brown. Let cool slightly. Dust with powdered sugar while still warm. Cool completely before cutting into bars.

CAKES

How sweet are thy words unto my taste!
yea, sweeter than honey to my mouth!

PSALM 119:103

Cake mixes from the store are easy to prepare and inexpensive…so why go to the trouble to bake your own from scratch? There are some good reasons, but probably the most important one is what you *won't* find in a homemade cake—things like hydrogenated fats, artificial flavors and colors, preservatives, additives, and loads of salt. You control what goes into your creations. And the flavor of a from-scratch cake can't be equaled. You have many tasty choices available to you in this chapter. With names like *Slush Cake, German Oat Cake,* or *Blueberry Streusel Cake,* to name just a few, you're bound to find some new family favorites.

Angel Food Cake

1 cup cake flour
½ cup powdered sugar
18 egg whites
⅛ tsp. salt
2 tsp. cream of tartar
1½ cups sugar
½ tsp. vanilla
½ tsp. almond extract

Chocolate Sauce
¼ cup butter
1 1-oz. square unsweetened chocolate
¾ cup sugar
⅛ tsp. salt
½ cup heavy cream
1 tsp. vanilla

Preheat oven to 350°. In a medium bowl, combine cake flour and powdered sugar. Set aside. In a large bowl, combine egg whites and salt. Beat until foamy. Add cream of tartar and continue beating until soft peaks form. Gradually add sugar and beat until stiff peaks form. Stir in vanilla and almond extracts. Fold in flour mixture and pour batter into a 10-inch tube pan. Bake 45 minutes. Invert and let cool completely before serving. Serve with chocolate sauce and fresh berries.

To make chocolate sauce, melt butter and chocolate together in a saucepan over low heat. Stir in sugar and salt until smooth. Add cream slowly and bring to boil. Remove from heat and stir in vanilla. Serve warm over angel food cake.

Apple Butter Cake

½ cup butter, softened
1 cup sugar
2 eggs, beaten
¾ cup apple butter
1 tsp. vanilla
2 cups all-purpose flour
½ cup rolled oats
1 tsp. baking powder
1 tsp. baking soda
½ tsp. salt
1 cup sour cream

Topping
1 cup brown sugar
1 tsp. cinnamon
½ tsp. nutmeg
½ cup chopped walnuts

Preheat oven to 350°. In a large bowl, cream butter and sugar until light and fluffy. Beat in eggs, apple butter, and vanilla. Set aside. In a separate bowl, combine flour, rolled oats, baking powder, baking soda, and salt. Stir dry ingredients into wet alternating with sour cream, beating well after each addition. Set aside.

To make topping, combine brown sugar, cinnamon, nutmeg, and chopped walnuts in a medium bowl. Pour half of cake batter into a greased and floured 9 x 13-inch pan. Sprinkle half the prepared topping over batter. Pour remaining batter over top and finish with remaining topping. Bake 35 to 40 minutes or until knife inserted into center comes out clean. Let cool before serving.

CAKES

Apple Cake

4 eggs
1¾ cups sugar
1 tsp. vanilla
¾ cup vegetable oil
2 cups all-purpose flour
½ tsp. salt
2 tsp. baking powder
2 tsp. baking soda
1 T. cinnamon, divided
½ tsp. nutmeg
5 baking apples, peeled, cored, and sliced
1 cup chopped walnuts
1 T. brown sugar

Preheat oven to 350°. In a large bowl, beat eggs, sugar, and vanilla until light and fluffy. Mix in oil and set aside. In a separate bowl, combine flour, salt, baking powder, baking soda, 2 teaspoons cinnamon, and nutmeg. Stir dry ingredients into wet. Fold in apples and walnuts and pour batter into a greased and floured 9 x 13-inch pan. In a small bowl, combine brown sugar and remaining teaspoon cinnamon. Sprinkle over cake. Bake 50 to 55 minutes or until a knife inserted into the center comes out clean. Let cool slightly before serving.

Apple Caramel Cake

2 large cooking apples
½ cup butter, softened to room temperature
1 cup sugar
1 egg
1 tsp. baking soda
¼ tsp. salt
1 tsp. cinnamon
1 scant tsp. nutmeg
1 cup all-purpose flour

½ cup pecans, measured and then finely chopped
sweetened whipped cream (optional)

Caramel Sauce
½ cup butter
1 cup brown sugar
½ tsp. salt
1 tsp. vanilla
½ cup evaporated milk

Peel, core, and chop apples into small pieces—you need
2½ cups total.

In a large mixing bowl, cream the butter. Add the sugar
and beat until fluffy. Add egg and beat until well blended.
Mix in the baking soda, salt, cinnamon, and nutmeg.
Add the flour and stir just until blended. Stir in apples
and pecans. Pour batter into a greased 9-inch round cake
pan. Bake in a preheated 350° oven 30 minutes or until
done.

While the cake is baking, prepare caramel sauce by melting the butter, brown sugar, and salt in a saucepan. Bring
to a boil while stirring with a whisk. Remove from heat
and stir in vanilla and milk. When ready to serve, ladle 2
to 3 tablespoons hot caramel sauce onto each plate. Cut
the cake into wedges and place the pieces on top of the
caramel sauce. Top with a dollop of sweetened whipped
cream if desired and serve warm.

CAKES

Banana Nut Cake

½ cup butter
1 cup sugar
¼ cup milk
2 eggs
1 tsp. vanilla
2 cups all-purpose flour
2 tsp. baking powder
1 tsp. baking soda
1 tsp. cream of tartar
¼ tsp. salt
1 cup mashed bananas
½ cup chopped walnuts

Preheat oven to 375°. In a large bowl, cream butter and sugar until smooth. Whisk in milk, eggs, and vanilla. Set aside. In a separate bowl, combine flour, baking powder, baking soda, cream of tartar, and salt. Stir dry ingredients into wet. Fold in mashed bananas and walnuts and pour batter into a greased and floured 9 x 13-inch pan. Bake 30 minutes or until knife inserted into center comes out clean.

Blueberry Cake

¼ cup butter
½ cup sugar
1 egg
1½ cups all-purpose flour
2½ tsp. baking powder
½ cup cream, divided
1 cup blueberries

Sauce
2 T. butter
1 cup sugar
¼ tsp. salt

CAKES

1 T. all-purpose flour
2 cups water
½ tsp. lemon extract

Preheat oven to 350°. In a large bowl, cream butter and sugar. Add egg and beat until fluffy. Set aside. In a separate bowl, combine flour and baking powder. Stir half of flour mixture into wet ingredients. Add ¼ cup cream and then add remaining flour mixture. Stir until combined. Add remaining ¼ cup cream to mixture. Gently fold in blueberries. Pour batter into a greased 8-inch square baking pan and bake 25 to 30 minutes or until golden.

To make sauce, melt butter in a saucepan over medium heat. Stir in sugar, salt, and flour until smooth. Pour in water and bring to a boil. Remove from heat and stir in lemon extract. Serve over warm blueberry cake.

Blueberry Streusel Cake

¾ cup sugar, divided
¼ cup butter, softened
1 tsp. grated lemon zest
1 egg
1½ cups plus 1 T. flour, divided
½ tsp. baking soda
½ cup plain yogurt
2 cups fresh blueberries
1 tsp. cinnamon
⅛ tsp. allspice
1 tsp. powdered sugar

In a large bowl, combine ½ cup of the sugar, butter, lemon zest, and egg and beat 5 minutes. Combine 1½ cups flour and baking soda. Add the flour mixture to the egg mixture alternately with the yogurt, using the lowest speed on your mixer.

CAKES

193

Grease the bottom and sides of a 9½-inch tart pan. Pour the batter into the prepared pan, spreading the batter over the bottom and up the sides of the pan.

Combine the remaining ¼ cup sugar, tablespoon of flour, blueberries, cinnamon, and allspice and mix gently to blend. Spoon berries over the batter leaving a ½-inch border around the edges.

Bake at 350° for 45 minutes or until lightly browned. Cool 20 minutes on a wire rack. Sprinkle with powdered sugar and serve.

Buttermilk Coffee Cake with Crumb Topping

2 cups all-purpose flour
2 cups brown sugar
1 tsp. baking powder
¼ tsp. salt
1 to 2 tsp. cinnamon
½ cup butter
1 cup buttermilk
1 tsp. baking soda
1 egg

Combine the flour, brown sugar, baking powder, salt, and cinnamon in a large bowl. Cut in the butter until the mixture resembles coarse crumbles. Set aside 1 cup of the crumbs for the topping.

Mix together the buttermilk and baking soda and then add the egg and mix again. Pour buttermilk mixture into the flour mixture and mix well. Pour batter into a greased 9 x 13-inch baking pan and sprinkle the reserved crumbs on top. Bake in a preheated 375° oven 20 minutes or until done. Best served warm.

Carrot Cake

4 eggs
1¼ cups vegetable oil
1 cup sugar
1 cup brown sugar
2 tsp. vanilla
2 cups all-purpose flour
1 tsp. baking soda
1 tsp. baking powder
½ tsp. salt
1 tsp. cinnamon
¼ tsp. nutmeg
3 cups grated carrots
1 cup chopped walnuts

Frosting
½ cup butter
1 8-oz. package cream cheese, softened
3½ cups powdered sugar
1 tsp. vanilla
½ cup chopped walnuts (optional)

Preheat oven to 350°. In a large bowl, beat together eggs, vegetable oil, sugar, brown sugar, and vanilla. Stir in flour, baking soda, baking powder, salt, cinnamon, and nutmeg. Fold in grated carrots and walnuts and stir well to combine. Pour batter into a greased 9 x 13-inch pan. Bake 40 to 50 minutes or until knife inserted into center comes out clean. Let cool completely before preparing frosting.

To make frosting, cream together butter and cream cheese. Stir in powdered sugar and vanilla until well combined. Spread over cake and garnish with walnuts if desired.

CAKES

Cherry Coffee Cake

1¾ cups all-purpose flour, divided
¾ cup sugar, divided
1 tsp. baking powder
¼ tsp. baking soda
¼ tsp. salt
½ cup plus 2 T. butter, melted
½ cup milk
1 egg
1 tsp. vanilla
¼ tsp. lemon extract or ½ tsp. lemon juice
1 21-oz. can cherry-pie filling (some cans are 22
    ounces, which is fine) or 1 qt. home canned

Preheat oven to 350°. Grease and flour a 9-inch square baking pan. In a large bowl and using a fork, mix 1¼ cups of the flour, ½ cup of the sugar, baking powder, baking soda, and salt.

In a small bowl, mix together ½ cup of the melted butter, milk, egg, and vanilla. Add to the flour mixture and using a wooden spoon, beat until well mixed. Pour batter into prepared baking pan.

In a small bowl and using a fork, combine ½ cup of the flour, ¼ cup of the sugar, and the remaining 2 tablespoons melted butter. Mix until coarse crumbles form. Sprinkle half of the crumb mixture over the batter.

Stir lemon extract or juice into the cherry pie filling and then spoon the fruit evenly over the crumb-topped batter in the pan. Sprinkle the fruit with the remaining crumb mixture. Bake 1 hour or until done.

Chocolate Applesauce Cake

½ cup shortening
¾ tsp. salt
½ tsp. each cinnamon, cloves, nutmeg, and allspice

2 T. cocoa powder
1½ cups sugar
2 eggs
2 cups sifted all-purpose flour
1½ tsp. baking soda
¾ cup chopped raisins
¾ cup chopped walnuts
1½ cups applesauce

In a large bowl, mix shortening, salt, spices, cocoa powder, sugar, and eggs together. In a separate bowl, add baking soda to flour and sift again. Add flour mixture to the egg mixture alternately with raisins, nuts, and applesauce. Pour batter into a greased and floured angel food cake tube pan. Bake at 350° for 50 to 55 minutes.

Chocolate Cake

½ cup butter
½ cup shortening
1 cup water
¼ cup cocoa powder
2 cups all-purpose flour
2 cups sugar
½ cup buttermilk
2 eggs
1 tsp. baking soda
1 tsp. vanilla

Frosting
6 T. butter
¼ cup milk
3 T. cocoa powder
3 cups powdered sugar
1 tsp. vanilla

Preheat oven to 400°. In a medium saucepan, combine butter, shortening, water, and cocoa powder. Bring to a boil over medium heat. Remove from heat and set aside. In a large bowl, combine flour, sugar, and buttermilk.

CAKES

Pour cocoa mixture over flour mixture and beat well to combine. Stir in eggs, baking soda, and vanilla. Pour batter into a greased and floured 9 x 13-inch pan. Bake 20 minutes or until a knife inserted into the center comes out clean. Let cake cool completely before frosting.

To make frosting, combine butter, milk, and cocoa powder in a saucepan. Bring to a boil and then remove from heat and beat in powdered sugar and vanilla. Mix until smooth. Spread frosting over cooled cake.

Chocolate Chiffon Cake

2 eggs, separated
1½ cups sugar, divided
1¾ cups cake flour
¾ tsp. baking soda
¾ tsp. salt
⅓ cup vegetable oil
1 cup buttermilk, divided
2 1-oz. squares unsweetened chocolate, melted

Preheat oven to 350°. In a large bowl, beat egg whites until frothy. Gradually beat in ½ cup sugar and whisk until egg whites form stiff peaks. Set aside. In a separate bowl, sift together remaining 1 cup sugar, cake flour, baking soda, and salt. Beat in vegetable oil and ½ cup buttermilk. When combined, mix in remaining ½ cup buttermilk, egg yolks, and melted chocolate. Mix thoroughly and fold in beaten egg whites. Bake in a 10-inch tube pan 40 to 45 minutes or until knife inserted into center comes out clean. Cool upright in pan on wire rack for 1 hour. Invert onto serving plate and let cool completely.

Christmas Cake

2 cups (4 sticks) butter
2¼ cups light brown sugar
6 eggs
4 cups all-purpose flour, sifted
1 tsp. baking powder
2 T. nutmeg
½ cup orange juice
1 lb. seedless golden raisins
3 cups chopped pecans

In a large bowl, cream together the butter and sugar. Add the eggs, 2 at a time, and beat until very light and mixture doesn't look grainy (takes about 20 minutes total). Sift together the flour, baking powder, and nutmeg. Add gradually to the creamed mixture and beat until well blended. Stir in the orange juice or blend in using lowest speed on mixer. Fold in the raisins and pecans.

Pour the cake batter into a greased and floured 10-inch tube pan. Bake at 300° for 1 hour and 45 minutes.

Remove from oven and cool for 10 minutes. Then turn the pan over and let cake slip out gently. Cool completely. Wrap tightly and store for at least a week before serving because it tends to be crumbly when fresh.

Coffee Cake

½ cup butter
1 cup sugar
½ cup brown sugar
1 cup sour cream
2 eggs
1 tsp. vanilla
2 cups all-purpose flour
1 tsp. baking powder
1 tsp. baking soda

CAKES

Filling
1 tsp. cinnamon
¼ cup brown sugar

Preheat oven to 350°. In a large bowl, cream butter, sugar, brown sugar, and sour cream. Beat in eggs and vanilla until smooth. Set aside. In a separate bowl, combine the flour, baking powder, and baking soda. Stir dry ingredients into wet. Set aside.

To make filling, combine cinnamon and brown sugar in a small bowl. Pour half of batter into tube pan. Sprinkle filling mixture over top. Pour remaining batter over filling and bake 45 to 50 minutes or until knife inserted into center comes out clean. Let cool completely before serving.

- -

Crumb Cake

½ cup butter, softened
1 cup sugar
1 egg
1 tsp. vanilla
2 cups all-purpose flour
1 tsp. baking powder
1 tsp. baking soda
¼ tsp. salt
½ tsp. nutmeg
1 cup buttermilk

Crumb Topping
½ cup all-purpose flour
½ cup brown sugar
¼ cup butter, softened
½ tsp. cinnamon

Preheat oven to 350°. To make cake, cream butter and sugar until light and fluffy in a large bowl. Stir in egg and vanilla and set aside. In a separate bowl, combine flour, baking powder, baking soda, salt, and nutmeg. Stir dry ingredients into wet. Mix in buttermilk and pour batter into a greased 9-inch square baking pan.

To make crumb topping, combine flour, brown sugar, butter, and cinnamon in a small bowl. Sprinkle topping over cake batter and bake 45 to 50 minutes or until knife inserted into center comes out clean. Let cool completely before serving.

Fresh Apple Cake

3 cups all-purpose flour
1 tsp. baking powder
1 tsp. baking soda
1½ tsp. salt
1 tsp. cinnamon
2 cups sugar
¾ cup vegetable oil
4 cups apples, peeled, cored, and chopped
2 eggs, beaten
1 cup nuts

In a large bowl, stir together the flour, baking powder, baking soda, salt, cinnamon, and sugar. Add the oil, apples, eggs, and nuts and stir until blended (the batter will seem dry). Bake in an ungreased angel food or Bundt cake pan at 350° for 1 hour and 15 minutes.

CAKES

Fudge Cake

1 cup water
1 cup butter
4 1-oz. squares unsweetened chocolate
2 cups all-purpose flour
2 cups sugar
½ tsp. baking soda
2 eggs
½ cup sour cream
1 tsp. vanilla
1 gallon vanilla ice cream

Preheat oven to 350°. In a small saucepan, heat water, butter, and chocolate, stirring constantly, until melted and smooth. Remove from heat and let cool. In a large bowl, combine the flour, sugar, and baking soda. Set aside. In a small bowl, beat together eggs, sour cream, and vanilla. Stir into flour mixture. Add cooled chocolate mixture and beat well to combine. Pour batter into a 10-inch tube pan and bake 50 to 55 minutes or until a knife inserted into the center comes out clean. Let cool 20 minutes, then serve warm with vanilla ice cream.

German Oat Cake

1¼ cups boiling water
1 cup rolled oats
4 oz. sweet baking chocolate bar
½ cup butter
1½ cups all-purpose flour
1 tsp. baking soda
3 eggs
1 tsp. vanilla
1 cup sugar
½ tsp. salt
1 cup packed brown sugar

Caramel Nut Topping
6 T. butter
2 T. corn syrup
¼ cup light cream (half-and-half)
¾ cup packed brown sugar
1 cup shredded coconut
1 cup chopped walnuts or pecans
1 tsp. vanilla

Pour boiling water over the oats, butter, and chocolate. Let stand for 20 minutes. Mix remaining ingredients together (except for the Caramel Nut Topping) in a large mixing bowl and then add the oats mixture and stir well. Pour batter into a greased and floured 9 x 13-inch pan and bake at 350° for 35-40 minutes or until done.

While the cake is baking, make the Caramel Nut Topping by combining the butter, corn syrup, light cream, and brown sugar in a small saucepan. Cook and stir until the mixture comes to a boil. Boil 2 minutes. Add remaining ingredients and then spread on warm cake. Set cake under a preheated broiler and broil about 5 inches from the heat until the topping is bubbly and golden brown.

- -

Gingerbread Cake

¼ cup butter
½ cup sugar
1 egg
¼ cup molasses
1 cup all-purpose flour
1 tsp. baking soda
1 tsp. ginger
½ tsp. cinnamon

Preheat oven to 350°. In a large bowl, cream butter and sugar. Add egg and beat until light and fluffy. Stir in molasses and set aside. In a separate bowl, combine flour,

CAKES

baking soda, ginger, and cinnamon. Stir flour mixture into wet ingredients and pour batter into a greased 9-inch square pan. Bake 40 minutes or until knife inserted into center comes out clean. Let cool.

Gold Cake

¾ cup butter
1¼ cups sugar
8 egg yolks
¼ tsp. lemon extract
2½ cups all-purpose flour
2½ tsp. baking powder
1 tsp. salt
¾ cup milk

Preheat oven to 350°. In a large bowl, cream butter and sugar until light and fluffy. Beat in egg yolks and lemon extract. Set aside. In a separate bowl, combine flour, baking powder, and salt. Add half of flour mixture into wet ingredients. Stir in milk and then mix in remaining flour mixture. Pour batter into a greased and floured 9-inch square pan. Bake 25 minutes or until golden. Let cool.

Half-Pound Cake

2 cups all-purpose flour
1½ cups sugar
4 eggs, room temperature
2 tsp. vanilla
2 tsp. baking powder
½ tsp. salt
1 cup butter, room temperature
½ cup milk
¼ tsp. mace

CAKES

In a large mixing bowl, put in all the ingredients at the same time. Beat on low until blended and then beat them on medium speed for 3 to 5 minutes. Pour the batter into a well-greased tube pan and place in the oven. Set the oven temperature to 350° and bake 1 hour. Remove cake from the oven and immediately invert the pan onto a wire rack. The cake should come right out, but if it doesn't, use a knife to loosen the cake from all the inside edges and then give it a good whack—it should come right out.

Holiday Gift Cake

1 cup butter
1 8-oz. package cream cheese, softened
1½ cups sugar
2 tsp. vanilla
½ tsp. almond extract
4 eggs
2¼ cups all-purpose flour
1½ tsp. baking powder
¾ cup chopped maraschino cherries
½ cup chopped pecans

Glaze
1½ cups powdered sugar
2 T. milk

Preheat oven to 325°. In a large bowl, cream butter and cream cheese until thoroughly blended. Mix in sugar, vanilla, and almond extract. Beat in eggs 1 at a time. Stir in flour and baking powder. Fold in cherries and pecans and pour batter into a greased and floured Bundt pan. Bake 1 hour and 20 minutes. Cool upright in pan on wire rack for 1 hour. Invert onto serving plate and let cool completely.

CAKES

To make glaze, combine powdered sugar and milk. Drizzle over cooled cake.

Mocha Pudding Cake

1 cup all-purpose flour
⅔ cup plus ⅓ cup sugar, divided
¼ cup plus 2 T. unsweetened cocoa powder, divided
1½ T. instant coffee granules
2 tsp. baking powder
¼ tsp. salt
½ cup milk
3 T. vegetable oil
1 tsp. vanilla
1 cup boiling water

Combine the flour, ⅔ cup of the sugar, ¼ cup of the unsweetened cocoa powder, instant coffee, baking powder, and salt in a large bowl. Stir well with a whisk. Combine milk, oil, and vanilla and add to the flour mixture. Stir until well blended.

Spoon batter into a greased 8 x 8-inch pan. Combine ⅓ cup of the sugar and 2 tablespoons unsweetened cocoa. Sprinkle over batter. Pour 1 cup boiling water over batter. Do not stir!

Bake in a preheated 350° oven 30 minutes. Serve warm with vanilla ice cream or sweetened whipped cream.

Nutmeg Cake

½ cup butter
1½ cups sugar
2 eggs
1 tsp. vanilla
2 cups all-purpose flour

¼ tsp. baking powder
½ tsp. nutmeg
½ cup milk
1 T. sugar
½ tsp. cinnamon

Preheat oven to 350°. In a large bowl, cream butter and sugar. Add eggs and vanilla and beat until fluffy. Set aside. In a separate bowl, combine flour, baking powder, and nutmeg. Stir half of dry ingredients into creamed mixture and then add half the milk. Add remaining flour mixture and remaining milk and mix well. Pour batter into a greased loaf pan and sprinkle top with sugar and cinnamon. Bake 40 to 45 minutes or until golden.

Oatmeal Cake

1 cup rolled oats, uncooked (don't use instant)
1½ cups boiling water
1½ cups all-purpose flour
½ tsp. baking soda
½ tsp. cinnamon
½ tsp. nutmeg
½ tsp. salt
½ cup butter, softened to room temperature
1 tsp. vanilla
1 cup brown sugar
1 cup sugar
2 eggs

Frosting
½ cup butter
1 cup brown sugar
1 5-ounce can evaporated milk
8 oz. flaked coconut
1 cup chopped pecans or walnuts
1 tsp. vanilla
small pinch of salt

Place the rolled oats in a small bowl and pour the boiling water over them. Let stand for 20 minutes.

In another small bowl, stir together the flour, baking soda, cinnamon, nutmeg, and salt. Set aside.

In a large mixing bowl, beat the butter until creamy. Add the vanilla and gradually add the sugars, beating until light and fluffy. Beat in the eggs 1 at a time. Add the oatmeal mixture and blend well. Pour batter into a greased 9 x 13-inch baking pan. Bake in a preheated 350° oven 35 minutes or until done. Remove from the oven and then turn the oven to broil.

While the cake is baking, prepare the frosting by melting butter in a large saucepan. Add the brown sugar and cook until the mixture boils and bubbles up. Add the evaporated milk and bring the mixture back to a boil. Remove from the heat and add the coconut, nuts, vanilla, and a very small pinch of salt. Keep frosting warm.

When the cake is done, spread the hot frosting on the hot cake. Broil the cake about 6 inches from the heat until the frosting bubbles all over the cake, about 2 minutes. Let cool somewhat before cutting because the frosting will cause burns if eaten too soon.

Orange Loaf Cake

2 cups all-purpose flour
1¼ cups sugar
1½ tsp. baking powder
1 tsp. salt
½ cup shortening
zest and juice of 1 orange
2 eggs

Preheat oven to 350°. In a large bowl, combine flour, sugar, baking powder, and salt. Cut in shortening with pastry blender until mixture resembles large crumbs. Set aside. Combine orange zest and juice and add enough water to equal ½ cup. Stir liquid into flour mixture and beat well. Whisk in eggs until well combined. Pour batter into a greased loaf pan and bake 1 hour or until golden. Let cool.

Peach Coffee Cake

1 cup sugar
½ cup butter
1 cup sour cream
1 tsp. vanilla
2 eggs
2 cups all-purpose flour
1½ tsp. baking powder
½ tsp. baking soda
½ tsp. salt
4 cups peeled and sliced peaches

Crumb Topping
¼ cup all-purpose flour
¼ cup sugar
¼ cup chopped pecans
1 tsp. cinnamon
3 T. cold butter

Preheat oven to 325°. In a large bowl, cream sugar and butter until light and fluffy. Beat in sour cream, vanilla, and eggs until smooth. Set aside. In a separate bowl, combine flour, baking powder, baking soda, and salt. Stir dry mixture into wet. Gently fold in peaches and pour batter into a greased and floured 9 x 13-inch baking pan. Set aside and prepare crumb topping. In a small bowl, combine flour, sugar, chopped pecans, and cinnamon. Cut in cold butter until mixture resembles coarse crumbs. Sprinkle crumb topping over batter in pan. Bake 45 minutes or until knife inserted into center comes out clean. Let cool completely before serving.

CAKES

Peach-Filled Coffee Cake

1½ cups all-purpose flour
1 cup sugar
2 tsp. baking powder
2 tsp. grated lemon zest
⅛ tsp. salt
1 cup butter, softened to room temperature
4 eggs
1 29-oz. can sliced peaches, well drained

Topping
½ cup butter
1 cup all-purpose flour
¼ cup sugar
1 T. grated lemon zest

Preheat oven to 350°. Grease a 9 x 13-inch baking pan.

In a large bowl, add the flour, sugar, baking powder, lemon zest, salt, butter, and eggs. Beat with an electric mixer at low speed until well blended. Then turn speed to medium and beat for 4 minutes. Spread batter evenly into the prepared baking pan. Evenly layer peaches on top of the batter.

To make topping, in a small saucepan, melt butter and then remove from heat. Stir in flour, sugar, and grated lemon zest until a soft, crumbly dough forms. Drop the pieces of dough on top of the peaches and bake 45 to 50 minutes or until light golden and done.

Pineapple Cake

2 cups all-purpose flour
2 cups sugar
2 tsp. baking soda
2 eggs, beaten
1 tsp. vanilla
1 20-oz. can crushed pineapple

Frosting
½ cup butter
1 8-oz. package cream cheese
1½ cups powdered sugar
1 tsp. vanilla
½ cup shredded coconut

Preheat oven to 350°. In a large bowl, mix together the flour, sugar, and baking soda. Stir in the beaten eggs, vanilla, and pineapple. Mix until well blended. Pour batter into a greased and floured 9 x 13-inch baking pan. Bake 45 minutes or until knife inserted into center comes out clean. Let cool 15 minutes before frosting.

To make frosting, cream butter and cream cheese. Mix in powdered sugar and vanilla until smooth. Stir in shredded coconut and spread over warm cake.

Pound Cake

1½ cups shortening
3 cups sugar
6 eggs
1 cup milk
3½ cups all-purpose flour
1 tsp. salt
1 tsp. vanilla
2 T. lemon extract

CAKES

Preheat oven to 350°. In a large bowl, cream shortening and sugar until fluffy. Beat in eggs 1 at a time, stirring well after each addition. Whisk in milk and set aside. In a separate bowl, combine flour and salt. Stir flour mixture into wet ingredients and beat to combine. Stir in vanilla and lemon extract. Pour batter into a 10-inch tube pan and bake 80 to 90 minutes or until knife inserted into center comes out clean. Let cool completely before serving.

Pumpkin Cake

⅔ cup butter
2¾ cups sugar
4 eggs
2 cups pumpkin
⅔ cup water
3½ cups all-purpose flour
½ tsp. baking powder
2 tsp. baking soda
1½ tsp. salt
1 tsp. cinnamon
½ tsp. cloves
½ cup chopped walnuts
½ cup raisins

Frosting
⅓ cup butter
1 cup brown sugar
¼ cup evaporated milk

Preheat oven to 350°. In a large bowl, cream butter and sugar. Beat in eggs until light and fluffy. Stir in pumpkin and water and whisk until well combined. Set aside. In a separate bowl, combine flour, baking powder, baking soda, salt, cinnamon, and cloves. Stir dry ingredients into wet and mix until combined. Fold in chopped walnuts and raisins. Pour batter into 2 greased loaf pans. Bake 1 hour or until knife inserted into center comes out clean.

Prepare frosting while cake is still hot. In a medium bowl, cream butter and brown sugar. Stir in evaporated milk. Spread over each cake and allow to cool.

Rhubarb Coffee Cake

½ cup shortening
1½ cups sugar
1 egg
1 tsp. vanilla
2 cups all-purpose flour
1 tsp. baking soda
½ tsp. salt
1 cup buttermilk
2 cups chopped fresh rhubarb

Filling
⅓ cup brown sugar
⅓ cup sugar
1 tsp. cinnamon
1 cup chopped walnuts

Preheat oven to 350°. Cream shortening and sugar in a large bowl. Beat in egg and vanilla until fluffy. Set aside. In a separate bowl, combine flour, baking soda, and salt. Gradually add flour mixture to wet ingredients, alternating with buttermilk. Mix well until batter is smooth. Fold chopped rhubarb into batter and set aside.

For filling, combine brown sugar, sugar, cinnamon, and chopped walnuts in a small bowl. Pour half of batter into a greased tube pan. Sprinkle filling mixture over batter. Pour remaining batter over filling. Bake 45 to 55 minutes or until knife inserted into center comes out clean. Let cool completely before serving.

CAKES

Salad Dressing Chocolate Cake

1 cup sugar
2 cups all-purpose flour
¼ cup cocoa powder
2 tsp. baking soda
¼ tsp. salt
1 cup Miracle Whip
1 cup cold water
1 tsp. vanilla

Preheat oven to 325°. In a large bowl, combine sugar, flour, cocoa powder, baking soda, and salt. Whisk in Miracle Whip, water, and vanilla. Pour batter into a greased 9-inch square pan and bake 35 minutes or until knife inserted into center comes out clean. Let cool.

Slush Cake

1 cup butter
2 cups all-purpose flour
1 cup chopped almonds
1 8-oz. package cream cheese
2 cups whipped dairy topping
1¾ cups powdered sugar, divided
2 tsp. orange zest (optional)
2 3-oz. packages instant chocolate pudding
3 cups milk
1½ pints heavy whipping cream

Preheat oven to 350°. To make first layer, use a pastry blender to combine butter, flour, and chopped almonds in a large bowl. Press into bottom of a greased 9 x 13-inch baking pan. Bake 30 minutes or until golden brown. Let cool completely before adding second layer.

To make second layer, mix cream cheese, whipped topping, 1½ cups powdered sugar, and orange zest, if using. Spread over top of cooled crust layer and refrigerate 30 minutes.

To make third layer, blend chocolate pudding and milk until smooth. Spread over top of cream cheese layer and refrigerate 30 minutes.

To make fourth layer, whip heavy cream and remaining ¼ cup powdered sugar until stiff peaks form. Spread over pudding layer. Refrigerate until ready to serve.

Spice Cake

2½ cups cake flour
1 tsp. baking powder
1 tsp. baking soda
¾ tsp. salt
¾ tsp. cinnamon
¾ tsp. cloves
⅔ cup brown sugar
1 cup sugar
½ cup shortening
2 eggs
1¼ cups buttermilk

Preheat oven to 375°. Sift cake flour, baking powder, baking soda, salt, cinnamon, cloves, brown sugar, and sugar together in a large bowl. Using a pastry blender, cut in shortening until mixture resembles coarse crumbs. Beat in eggs and buttermilk until well combined. Pour batter into a greased 9 x 13-inch baking dish. Bake 30 to 35 minutes or until knife inserted into center comes out clean. Let cool before serving.

CAKES

Sponge Cake

6 eggs, separated
1 cup sugar
¼ cup water
1 tsp. lemon extract
1 tsp. lemon zest
1 cup cake flour
½ tsp. cream of tartar
¼ tsp. salt

Preheat oven to 325°. In a large bowl, beat egg yolks until thick and lemon-colored. Beat in sugar until combined. Whisk in water, lemon extract, and lemon zest until smooth. Stir in flour and set aside. In a separate bowl, beat egg whites until foamy. Mix in cream of tartar and salt. Beat until egg whites form stiff peaks. Fold whites into yolk mixture. Pour batter into a tube pan and bake 1 hour or until knife inserted into center comes out clean. Let cool completely before serving.

Tunnel of Fudge Cake

1¾ cups butter, softened
1¾ cups sugar
6 eggs
2 cups powdered sugar
2¼ cups all-purpose flour
¾ cup cocoa powder
½ tsp. salt
2 cups chopped walnuts

Glaze
¾ cup powdered sugar
¼ cup cocoa powder
2 T. milk

Preheat oven to 350°. In a large bowl, beat butter and sugar until light and fluffy. Add eggs 1 at a time, beating well after each addition. Gradually add powdered sugar, blending well. Stir in flour, cocoa powder, salt, and walnuts until well combined. Spoon batter into a greased and floured Bundt pan or 10-inch tube pan. Bake 1 hour. Cool upright in pan on wire rack for 1 hour. Invert onto serving plate and let cool completely.

To make glaze, combine powdered sugar, cocoa powder, and milk. Drizzle over cooled cake.

Two-Egg Cake

2 cups cake flour
1⅓ cups sugar
2½ tsp. baking powder
½ cup butter, melted
1 cup milk, divided
1 tsp. vanilla
2 eggs

Preheat oven to 350°. In a large bowl, stir together cake flour, sugar, and baking powder. Stir in melted butter, ¾ cup milk, and vanilla. Beat well and then add eggs and remaining ¼ cup milk. Pour batter into a greased 9-inch square pan and bake 45 to 50 minutes. Let cool.

CAKES

Walnut Cake

½ cup butter
1½ cups sugar
1½ tsp. vanilla
2 cups all-purpose flour
1 tsp. baking soda
1 tsp. cream of tartar
¾ tsp. salt
¾ cup milk
1 cup chopped walnuts
4 egg whites

Preheat oven to 350°. In a large bowl, cream butter, sugar, and vanilla. Set aside. In a separate bowl, sift together flour, baking soda, cream of tartar, and salt. Stir half into creamed ingredients. Whisk in milk and then add remaining flour mixture. Mix in walnuts. In a separate bowl, beat egg whites until they form stiff peaks. Gently fold whites into batter. Pour batter into a greased loaf pan and bake 45 to 50 minutes or until knife inserted into center comes out clean. Let cool before serving.

White Fruit Cake

1 cup butter
½ tsp. lemon extract
½ tsp. vanilla
¼ tsp. salt
2 cups sugar
4 eggs
½ cup milk
4 cups all-purpose flour, divided
1 tsp. baking powder
½ cup golden raisins
1 cup currants
1 cup chopped walnuts
¼ cup green candied cherries

½ cup red candied cherries
½ cup candied pineapple
1 T. orange zest
1 T. lemon zest

Preheat oven to 350°. In a large bowl, cream butter and stir in lemon and vanilla extracts. Stir in salt and sugar. When combined, add eggs 1 at a time, beating well after each addition. Whisk in milk and then stir in 3½ cups flour and baking powder. Set aside. In a separate bowl, mix remaining ½ cup flour with golden raisins, currants, walnuts, green and red candied cherries, candied pineapple, orange zest, and lemon zest. Stir fruit and nuts into batter. Pour batter into a greased and floured Bundt pan and bake 1 hour or until golden. Cool upright in pan on wire rack for 1 hour. Invert onto serving plate and let cool completely before serving.

- -

Yellow Cake

⅔ cup shortening
1½ cups sugar
3 eggs
1 tsp. vanilla
2 cups all-purpose flour
2 tsp. baking powder
½ tsp. salt
⅓ cup milk

Chocolate Icing
¼ cup butter
1 cup sugar
⅓ cup milk
1 1-oz. square unsweetened chocolate, chopped
⅛ tsp. salt
1 tsp. vanilla

CAKES

Preheat oven to 350°. In a large bowl, cream shortening and sugar. Add eggs and vanilla and beat well to combine. Set aside. In a separate bowl, combine flour, baking powder, and salt. Stir half of flour mixture into wet ingredients. Mix in milk and then stir in remaining flour mixture. Beat well to combine. Pour batter into 2 greased 8-inch square pans and bake 25 to 30 minutes. Let cool before preparing chocolate icing.

To make chocolate icing, combine butter, sugar, milk, chopped chocolate, and salt in a medium saucepan. Cook, stirring frequently, over medium-low heat. Bring to a boil and let simmer 2 minutes. Remove from heat and stir in vanilla. Let cool. Beat thoroughly and spread over cooled cake.

PIES, COBBLERS, AND CRISPS

Let the field be joyful, and all that is therein:
then shall all the trees of the wood rejoice.

Psalm 96:2

Nothing says *love* like a warm, bubbling pie fresh out of the oven. Making homemade pie may look difficult, but with patience, confidence, and practice you'll be an expert in no time. There's a pie here for every occasion—chocolate pie for a winter night, Fourth of July berry pie for a summer picnic, cheesecake for a special birthday, apple pie for Thanksgiving, and all sorts of pies for the ordinary days in between!

Best Piecrust

Single Crust
1 scant cup all-purpose flour
½ scant tsp. salt
2 T. ice water
6 T. cold shortening

Double Crust
1¾ cups all-purpose flour
¾ tsp. salt
¼ cup ice water
¾ cup cold shortening

In a large bowl, stir flour and salt together with fork. Set aside ¼ cup of this mixture for single crust or ½ cup for double crust. Mix with ice water to create a thin paste. Set aside. With pastry blender, combine shortening with remaining flour mixture until crumbs are the size of large peas. Create a well in center of dough and add the paste. Using hands, form dough into large ball (or 2 balls if making double crust). Press into a 6-inch-wide round. Cover with plastic wrap and chill 30 minutes. Roll out on floured surface and lay in pie plate.

Note: This dough freezes well. Cover 6-inch rounds in plastic wrap, store in freezer bag, and place in freezer for up to 6 months. The day before using, thaw rounds in refrigerator. When thawed, roll out as usual.

Gingersnap Crust

1¼ cups crushed gingersnaps
⅓ cup finely chopped walnuts
⅓ cup butter, melted
⅓ cup brown sugar

Preheat oven to 350°. Combine all ingredients in a medium bowl. Using a rubber spatula or fingers, press into a 9-inch pie plate. Bake 8 to 10 minutes. Let cool completely before filling.

Graham Cracker Crust

1¼ cups graham cracker crumbs
¼ cup sugar
6 T. butter, melted

Preheat oven to 375°. Combine all ingredients in a medium bowl. Using a rubber spatula or fingers, press into a 9-inch pie plate. Bake 6 to 8 minutes. Let cool completely before filling.

Note: Vanilla wafers may be substituted for graham crackers.

Prebaked Piecrust

1¼ cups all-purpose flour
½ tsp. salt
1 T. sugar
6 T. butter, chilled and cut into ¼-inch cubes
¼ cup chilled shortening
3 to 4 T. ice water

Combine flour, salt, and sugar in a medium bowl. Using a pastry blender, cut in the butter and shortening until mixture resembles coarse crumbs. Sprinkle ice water over mixture 1 tablespoon at a time until dough just begins to clump together. Gather dough into large ball, cover with plastic wrap, and freeze 30 to 60 minutes. Roll out on floured surface and place in a pie plate. Return to freezer and chill an additional 15 minutes.

Preheat oven to 350°. Line crust with parchment paper and fill with pie weights. Bake 20 minutes. Remove pie weights and parchment paper. Poke several small holes in bottom of crust with fork. Return to oven 10 additional minutes. Let cool before filling.

Note: If the edges are drying out or burning before the crust has finished baking, tent them with aluminum foil.

Apple Crisp

Apple Filling
¼ cup sugar
½ tsp. cinnamon
¼ tsp. nutmeg
¼ tsp. cloves
6 tart apples, peeled, cored, and sliced
2 tsp. lemon juice

Crumb Topping
½ cup sugar
½ cup all-purpose flour
¼ tsp. salt
½ cup rolled oats
½ tsp. cinnamon
½ tsp. nutmeg
6 T. butter
¼ cup chopped nuts (optional)

Preheat oven to 350°. To make apple filling, combine sugar, cinnamon, nutmeg, and cloves in a large bowl. Add apples and sprinkle lemon juice over top. Toss gently until apples are coated in sugar mixture. Pour into a greased 9 x 13-inch baking dish.

To make crumb topping, combine sugar, flour, salt, rolled oats, cinnamon, and nutmeg in a medium bowl. Using a fork or pastry blender, cut in butter until mixture is crumbly. Toss in nuts if desired. Spread crumb topping evenly over apples. Bake 45 minutes or until crumb topping is golden brown. Let cool at least 15 minutes before serving.

Apple Crumb Pie

Filling
6 cups peeled, sliced apples
2/3 cup sugar
2 T. all-purpose flour
1 tsp. cinnamon
1 single piecrust, unbaked

Topping
½ cup brown sugar
1 cup flour
½ cup butter, chilled

Mix together the first 4 filling ingredients and pour into the unbaked piecrust.

To make the topping, combine the brown sugar and flour and then cut in the butter, mixing until it resembles coarse crumbles. Spoon the topping over the apple pie filling and pat down gently to help keep the crumbs from falling off the edge of the pie.

Bake in a preheated 350° oven 1 hour.

Apple Pear Crumble

1½ cups rolled oats
½ cup all-purpose flour
1 cup brown sugar, divided
½ cup butter
2 cups peeled and diced apples
2 cups peeled and diced pears
1 T. lemon juice
½ tsp. salt
1 tsp. cinnamon
½ cup chopped walnuts

Preheat oven to 350°. In a large bowl, combine oats, flour, and ½ cup brown sugar. Cut in butter until crumbly. Set aside. In separate bowl, combine apples, pears, lemon juice, salt, cinnamon, and remaining ½ cup brown sugar. Spread apple-pear mixture in bottom of a greased 9-inch square baking dish. Sprinkle oat mixture over apple-pear mixture and top with chopped walnuts. Bake 40 minutes or until golden. Serve warm.

Apple Pie

½ cup sugar
½ cup brown sugar
2 T. all-purpose flour
⅛ tsp. salt
½ tsp. cinnamon
¼ tsp. nutmeg
¼ tsp. allspice
5 large Granny Smith apples, peeled, cored, and sliced
2 T. butter, cubed
double piecrust, unbaked

Preheat oven to 400°. In a large bowl, combine sugar, brown sugar, flour, salt, cinnamon, nutmeg, and allspice. Add sliced apples and toss gently to coat. Pour mixture into piecrust and dot with small cubes of butter. Cover with top crust and brush with egg wash if desired. Cut steam vents and bake 35 to 40 minutes or until juices begin to bubble. Let cool completely before serving.

- -

Apple Turnovers

2 cups all-purpose flour
1 tsp. salt
1 cup butter, divided
½ cup ice water
2 apples, peeled, cored, and sliced
½ cup sugar
1 T. cornstarch
1 tsp. lemon juice
¼ tsp. cinnamon
1 egg
2 T. water, divided
½ cup powdered sugar

In a medium mixing bowl, combine the flour and salt. Add ½ cup of the butter and, using a pastry cutter or 2 butter knives, cut in the butter until mixture resembles coarse crumbles. Sprinkle with the ice water and mix well with a fork. Shape dough into a ball and then turn out onto a lightly floured surface. Lightly flour a rolling pin and roll dough into an 18 x 8-inch rectangle. Cut ¼ cup of the butter into very thin, small pieces. Lay the pieces on ⅔ of the dough, leaving ½ inch of space around edges (you will have butter pieces on 8 x 12 inches of the rectangle). Fold the unbuttered third of dough over the middle third and then fold the remaining (buttered) dough over the middle to make a 3-layer "package" about 8 x 6 inches. Now, roll out the dough again into an 18 x 8-inch rectangle and, using the last ¼ cup of the butter, repeat the process, dotting ⅔ of the rectangle with butter and then folding by thirds. Wrap the dough package with plastic wrap and chill in the refrigerator for 15 minutes. Remove the dough and roll again into an 18 x 8-inch rectangle. Fold the dough in half lengthwise, and then in half widthwise, wrap in plastic wrap, and chill in the refrigerator for 1 hour.

Meanwhile, prepare the filling. In a saucepan, mix together the apples, sugar, cornstarch, lemon juice, and cinnamon. Cook, stirring frequently, until apples are tender. Chill.

Preheat oven to 450°.

Cut dough in half and place the half you're not working with back in the refrigerator to keep cold. Roll out dough half into a 12-inch square and then cut into four 6-inch squares.

In a cup or small bowl, beat the egg with 1 tablespoon water. Brush the egg mixture over each of the squares and then spoon ⅛ of the apple mixture into the center of each square. Fold squares in half and then pinch and press edges to seal. Chill turnovers while preparing the other half of the batch.

Lay the turnovers on a baking sheet, leaving plenty of room between them. Brush turnovers with the egg mixture. Cut 2 small slashes on the top of each turnover. Bake 20 minutes or until done. Cool on wire rack.

While the turnovers are cooling, mix together 1 tablespoon water and the powdered sugar in a small bowl. Drizzle glaze over the cooled turnovers. (Although I think these are excellent without the glaze, it's cook's choice.)

Apricot Pie

1 cup dried apricots
1 cup orange juice
1 T. honey
1 tsp. lemon juice
½ tsp. lemon zest
1 cup sugar, divided
⅛ tsp. salt
3 egg whites
½ tsp. cream of tartar
dash nutmeg
single piecrust, prebaked

Roughly chop dried apricots. Place in a medium saucepan and add orange juice and honey. Cook on medium heat, stirring occasionally, until fruit is very tender and liquid thickens, about 30 minutes.

Preheat oven to 325°. Pour apricot mixture into a large bowl and stir in lemon juice, lemon zest, ¾ cup sugar, and salt. Set aside. In a separate bowl, beat egg whites until stiff. Fold in remaining ¼ cup sugar, cream of tartar, and nutmeg. Fold egg white mixture into apricot mixture. Pour into prebaked piecrust and bake 20 to 25 minutes or until apricot filling is bubbly.

Banana Cream Pie

¾ cup sugar
⅓ cup all-purpose flour
¼ tsp. salt
2 cups milk
3 egg yolks, lightly beaten
2 T. butter
2 tsp. vanilla
4 bananas, sliced
single piecrust, prebaked
sweetened whipped cream

Preheat oven to 350°. In a medium saucepan, whisk together the sugar, flour, and salt. Whisk in the milk gradually and cook over medium heat, stirring constantly, until mixture begins to bubble. Cook an additional 2 minutes and then remove from heat.

Stir ¼ cup of the hot mixture into the beaten egg yolks. Add egg yolk mixture back into the saucepan. Cook 2 minutes longer, stirring constantly. Remove from heat and stir in butter and vanilla. Pour through a fine-mesh strainer to remove any lumps.

Arrange banana slices over bottom of cooled prebaked crust, reserving several slices for garnish. Pour custard mixture over top of bananas. Bake 12 to 15 minutes. Remove from oven and let cool 15 minutes. Refrigerate until ready to serve, at least 1 hour. Garnish pie with sweetened whipped cream and additional banana slices just before serving.

Black Raspberry Cobbler

4 to 5 cups black raspberries
½ cup sugar
½ cup brown sugar
2 T. all-purpose flour
¼ cup butter, cut into small pieces
2 T. lemon juice
½ tsp. nutmeg
additional sugar and nutmeg for sprinkling

Dough
1½ cups all-purpose flour
3 T. sugar
1½ tsp. baking powder
1 tsp. salt
½ cup butter, chilled
½ cup milk, more or less
½ tsp. vanilla

Grease a 1½-quart casserole and place the raspberries in the greased pan. Add the sugars and flour and toss gently to mix. Dot with butter. Sprinkle with lemon juice and nutmeg. Bake in a preheated 350° oven 15 minutes.

Meanwhile, make the dough by mixing together the flour, sugar, baking powder, and salt in a medium-size mixing bowl. Cut in the chilled butter until mixture resembles coarse crumbles. Combine the milk and vanilla and gradually add to the flour mixture. Using a fork, stir until a ball forms, adding more milk only if necessary. Turn out dough ball onto a floured surface and roll dough to ¼-inch thickness. Shape the dough to fit the casserole dish you are using and place the dough over the warm fruit. Slash a cross in the center to vent steam and continue baking for 30 to 40 minutes or until the juices bubble up through the slit and the crust is flaky and golden.

Blackberry Cobbler

1 qt. blackberries
1¼ cups sugar
2 T. flour
2 T. butter, cubed
1½ cups all-purpose flour
1½ tsp. baking powder
¼ tsp. salt
2 T. sugar
¼ cup butter
⅔ cup milk
1 egg, beaten

Preheat oven to 400°. Toss blackberries with 1¼ cups sugar and 2 tablespoons flour. Spread into a greased 9-inch square baking dish and dot with butter. Set aside. Whisk together the flour, baking powder, salt, and 2 tablespoons sugar. Using a pastry blender, cut in ¼ cup butter until mixture resembles coarse crumbs. Stir in milk and beaten egg until combined. Drop batter over berries and bake until golden, 20 to 30 minutes. Let cool at least 30 minutes before serving.

Blueberry Pie

3½ cups fresh blueberries
1 cup sugar
1 T. lemon juice
2 T. cornstarch
double piecrust, unbaked
1 T. butter, cut into cubes
¼ tsp. nutmeg
¼ tsp. cinnamon

In a large bowl, combine blueberries, sugar, lemon juice, and cornstarch. Let stand about 20 minutes for juices to distribute.

Preheat oven to 425°. Pour blueberries into unbaked pie shell. Dot with pieces of butter and sprinkle nutmeg and cinnamon over top. Place top crust over berries and cut steam vents. Bake 10 minutes and then reduce heat to 325° and bake 30 minutes longer. Let cool completely before serving.

Bob and Andy Pie

1 cup sugar
1 cup brown sugar
2 T. all-purpose flour
½ tsp. cinnamon
¼ tsp. cloves
¼ tsp. salt
3 eggs

2 cups milk
1 T. butter, melted
1 tsp. vanilla
single piecrust, unbaked

Preheat oven to 350°. In a large bowl, blend sugar, brown sugar, flour, cinnamon, cloves, and salt.

In a separate bowl, beat the eggs until frothy. Add the milk, butter, and vanilla and stir to blend thoroughly. Blend milk mixture into the flour mixture and stir to thoroughly combine. Pour into the unbaked pie shell.

Bake 45 minutes. The pie will be puffed up when it first comes from the oven but will collapse as it cools. Serve at room temperature or just barely warm.

Brown Sugar Pie

3 cups brown sugar, packed
¼ cup all-purpose flour
⅛ tsp. salt
3 eggs, lightly beaten
½ tsp. vanilla
1½ cups milk
single piecrust, unbaked

Preheat oven to 350°. In a large bowl, combine brown sugar, flour, and salt. Stir in eggs and vanilla until combined. Gradually whisk in milk. Pour mixture into an unbaked piecrust. Bake 30 minutes. Let cool until ready to serve.

PIES, COBBLERS, AND CRISPS

Buttermilk Pie

1 cup sugar
3 T. flour
dash salt
2 egg yolks, lightly beaten
2 cups buttermilk
½ tsp. vanilla
1 T. butter, melted
single piecrust, unbaked
dash nutmeg

Preheat oven to 450°. In a large bowl, combine sugar, flour, and salt. Beat in egg yolks, then gradually whisk in buttermilk. Add vanilla and melted butter. Pour mixture into an unbaked piecrust and sprinkle nutmeg over top. Bake 15 minutes. Reduce oven temperature to 350° and cook 30 minutes longer or until a knife inserted into the center comes out clean. Let cool completely before serving.

Butterscotch Pie

1½ cups milk
1 cup brown sugar
¼ cup all-purpose flour
¼ tsp. salt
3 egg yolks
3 T. butter
½ tsp. vanilla
single piecrust, unbaked

Preheat oven to 325°. Combine milk, brown sugar, flour, and salt in the top of a double boiler. Place over boiling water and cook, stirring constantly, until the mixture begins to thicken, about 8 minutes. Remove from heat and set aside.

Beat egg yolks in a small bowl. Pour ½ cup of the hot mixture into the yolks and immediately return egg mixture to saucepan. Cook until thick. Remove from heat and stir butter and vanilla into custard. Pour mixture into an unbaked single piecrust. Bake 10 to 12 minutes. Let cool completely before serving.

Caramel Apple Pie

Taffy
½ cup brown sugar
¼ cup butter, melted
⅓ cup all-purpose flour

Apple Filling
⅔ cup sugar
3 T. all-purpose flour
2 tsp. cinnamon
5 Granny Smith apples, peeled, cored, and sliced
1 tsp. lemon juice
20 caramels, halved
double piecrust, unbaked
vanilla ice cream (to serve)

Preheat oven to 375°. To make taffy, combine brown sugar, melted butter, and ⅓ cup flour. Set aside.

To make apple filling, combine sugar, flour, and cinnamon in a large bowl. Add sliced apples and sprinkle with lemon juice. Toss gently to coat. Spoon half of apple filling into piecrust. Top with half the caramels and half the taffy mixture. Add remaining apple mixture and finish with remaining caramels and taffy. Cover with top crust and brush with egg wash if desired. Cut steam vents and bake 45 to 50 minutes or until crust is golden. Let cool 30 minutes and serve warm with vanilla ice cream.

PIES, COBBLERS, AND CRISPS

Carrot Pie

2 cups chopped carrots
¾ cup sugar
2 eggs
⅛ tsp. salt
1 tsp. cinnamon
¼ tsp. ginger
¼ tsp. allspice
¼ tsp. cloves
¼ tsp. mace (optional)
1 tsp. vanilla
¾ cup milk
single piecrust, unbaked

Preheat oven to 400°. In a saucepan, add chopped carrots and enough water to cover. Bring to a boil and simmer until tender, about 10 minutes. Drain well and then mash carrots until smooth with a potato masher/ricer.

In a mixing bowl, mix together the mashed carrots, sugar, eggs, and salt. Add the spices and vanilla and mix well again. Gradually stir in milk, mixing as you pour. Mix well again.

Pour into an unbaked piecrust, place the pie in the oven, and bake 10 minutes. Turn down heat to 350° and continue baking 40 to 45 additional minutes or until the pie is firm.

Cheesecake

Crust
1 cup graham cracker crumbs
¼ cup chopped walnuts
3 T. brown sugar
2 tsp. cinnamon
½ tsp. nutmeg
5 T. butter, melted

Filling
3 8-oz. packages cream cheese
1 cup sugar
1 cup sour cream
1 cup heavy cream
3 T. all-purpose flour
1 T. vanilla
1 T. lemon juice
2 tsp. lemon zest
3 eggs
fresh fruit or berries (to serve)

Preheat oven to 325°. To make crust, combine graham cracker crumbs, chopped walnuts, brown sugar, cinnamon, nutmeg, and melted butter in a medium bowl. Mix well and press into the bottom of a 9-inch springform pan. Bake 10 minutes. Remove from oven and set aside.

To make filling, beat cream cheese and sugar together in a large bowl until smooth. Beat in sour cream and heavy cream. Add in flour, vanilla, lemon juice, and lemon zest. Stir in eggs 1 at a time, beating well after each addition. Pour filling over crust and bake 60 minutes. Turn off oven and open oven door. Let cake cool in oven 30 minutes, then remove and run a knife around the edge. Let cool completely on counter, then refrigerate until ready to serve. Serve with fresh fruit or berries.

PIES, COBBLERS, AND CRISPS

Cherry Cobbler

1 qt. tart "pie" cherries, washed and pitted
1 cup plus 2 T. sugar
¼ cup brown sugar
2 T. minute tapioca
½ tsp. almond extract
1½ cups all-purpose flour
2 tsp. baking powder
½ tsp. salt
6 T. butter, chilled
1 egg
⅓ cup milk
½ tsp. nutmeg

In a 7 x 12-inch baking dish or 2-quart casserole, combine the cherries, 1 cup of the sugar, the brown sugar, tapioca, and almond extract. Set aside while you prepare the batter.

In a large mixing bowl, stir together the flour, baking powder, and salt. Cut in ¼ cup of the butter until coarse crumbles form. In a small bowl, beat together the egg and milk. Stir into the flour mixture just until blended. Dot the cherries with the remaining 2 tablespoons butter. Drop the batter in 6 equal mounds over the top of the cherries. In a small bowl, mix together the remaining 2 tablespoons sugar with the nutmeg. Sprinkle on top of the batter.

Bake in a preheated 400° oven 25 to 35 minutes or until the fruit is bubbling up in the middle of the pan and the dumplings are golden.

Cherry-Rhubarb Pie

2 cups sour cherries, pitted
2 cups chopped rhubarb
¼ cup all-purpose flour

1½ cups sugar
1 tsp. almond extract
2 T. butter, chopped
double piecrust, unbaked

Preheat oven to 425°. In a large bowl, combine cherries, rhubarb, flour, sugar, and almond extract. Set aside 20 minutes to let juices distribute. Pour into pie shell and dot with cubes of butter. Cover with top crust and brush with egg wash if desired. Cut several steam vents. Bake 45 to 50 minutes or until juices begin to bubble and crust is golden.

Chocolate Pie

1½ cups sugar
3 T. cornstarch
½ tsp. salt
2 cups milk
1 cup heavy cream
3 1-oz. chocolate squares, chopped
3 egg yolks, lightly beaten
1 T. butter
2 tsp. vanilla
single piecrust, prebaked
whipped cream, to serve

Combine sugar, cornstarch, and salt in a large saucepan. Gradually stir in milk, heavy cream, and chopped chocolate. Cook over medium heat, stirring constantly, until mixture thickens and boils. Remove from heat. Stir ½ cup of the hot mixture into the beaten egg yolks and then pour egg mixture into the pan. Boil 1 minute longer, stirring constantly. Remove from heat and blend in butter and vanilla. Pour mixture through a fine-mesh strainer to remove any lumps. Pour immediately into baked crust. Chill until firm, at least 4 hours. Serve with whipped cream.

PIES, COBBLERS, AND CRISPS

Chocolate Strawberry Pie

3 1-oz squares semisweet chocolate, divided
1 T. butter
single piecrust, prebaked
6 oz. cream cheese, softened
½ cup sour cream
3 T. sugar
½ tsp. vanilla
4 cups fresh strawberries, hulled
⅓ cup strawberry jam, melted

Melt 2 squares of chocolate and butter over low heat. Brush over bottom and sides of prebaked piecrust. Refrigerate until firm, about 15 minutes. Meanwhile, beat cream cheese, sour cream, sugar, and vanilla in a large bowl. When smooth, spread over chocolate layer using a rubber spatula. Press a sheet of plastic wrap over top and chill at least 2 hours. Arrange hulled strawberries on top of the filling with the bottoms pointing up. Brush melted jam over berries. Melt remaining chocolate square and drizzle over pie. Chill until ready to serve.

Cranberry Walnut Pie

4 cups cranberries
¼ cup water
1½ cups sugar
1 T. cornstarch mixed with 1 T. water
¼ cup light corn syrup
1 tsp. orange zest
2 T. fresh orange juice
¼ tsp. salt
1 T. butter
1 cup chopped walnuts
double piecrust, unbaked

Preheat oven to 425°. Combine cranberries, water, and sugar in a medium saucepan. Cook over medium heat, stirring constantly, until mixture comes to a boil. Stir in cornstarch and corn syrup and cook, stirring constantly, until mixture begins to thicken. Stir in orange zest, orange juice, salt, and butter. Return to a boil. Fold in walnuts. Remove saucepan from heat and let mixture cool for 5 minutes. Pour mixture into crust. Cover with top crust and cut several steam vents. Brush with egg wash if desired and bake 25 to 30 minutes. Let cool completely before serving.

- -

Currant Pie

double piecrust, unbaked
3 cups fresh currants
2 cups sugar
¼ cup instant tapioca
1 tsp. almond extract
small pinch salt
3 T. butter
sugar for sprinkling

Line the bottom of your pie plate with half of the pastry dough, making sure it is large enough to go completely up the sides and slightly over the edge.

In a large bowl, combine the currants, sugar, tapioca, almond extract, and salt. Pour fruit mixture into the pie shell and then dot the top of the fruit with the butter. Roll out the other half of the pie dough and set on top. Crimp edges of top and bottom crust together, fluting the edge. Slash a cross or several slits across the top of the piecrust to allow steam to vent. Sprinkle with sugar.

Bake in a preheated 350° oven 45 minutes or until the pie is done and the juices bubble up through the vent.

Custard Pie

4 eggs
¾ cup sugar
1¼ tsp. vanilla
¼ tsp. salt
2½ cups milk, scalded
single piecrust, unbaked
nutmeg for dusting

Preheat oven to 350°. In a large mixing bowl, combine the eggs, sugar, vanilla, and salt. Beat thoroughly. Gradually add 1 cup of the scalded milk to the egg mixture, beating on low the entire time. Add the rest of the milk and continue to beat on low. Pour the custard into the unbaked pie shell and sprinkle the top with nutmeg.

Bake on the lowest shelf of the oven 40 minutes or until it is done and looks golden. Allow to cool to room temperature before cutting and serving.

Dutch Apple Pie

Apple Filling
3 T. all-purpose flour
⅔ cup sugar
½ tsp. cinnamon
¼ tsp. nutmeg
¼ tsp. allspice
5 Granny Smith apples, peeled, cored, and sliced
2 T. butter, cubed
single piecrust, unbaked

Crumb Topping
¾ cup all-purpose flour
½ tsp. cinnamon
½ cup brown sugar
¾ cup rolled oats
½ cup butter

Preheat oven to 425°. To make apple filling, combine flour, sugar, cinnamon, nutmeg, and allspice in a large bowl. Add apples and toss until evenly coated. Pour apples into piecrust and dot with small cubes of butter. Cover lightly with aluminum foil and bake 10 minutes.

While filling is baking, prepare crumb topping. In a medium bowl, combine flour, cinnamon, brown sugar, and rolled oats. Using a pastry blender, cut in butter until crumbs are the size of large peas. Remove pie from oven and sprinkle crumbs over top. Reduce oven temperature to 375° and bake 30 to 35 minutes longer, until crumb topping has browned. Let cool completely before serving.

Fourth of July Berry Pie

Crust
½ cup butter, softened
¾ cup sugar
1 egg
1¼ cups all-purpose flour
1 tsp. cream of tartar
½ tsp. baking soda
¼ tsp. salt

Filling
½ cup marshmallow crème
8 oz. cream cheese, softened
½ cup sugar
2 tsp. vanilla
1 cup fresh blueberries
1 cup sliced fresh strawberries

Preheat oven to 350°. To make crust, cream butter and sugar until smooth. Beat in egg and set aside. In a separate bowl, combine flour, cream of tartar, baking soda, and salt. Stir dry ingredients into wet. Using floured

PIES, COBBLERS, AND CRISPS

hands, press dough onto a 12-inch pizza pan. Bake 15 to 17 minutes. Let cool.

When crust is cool, cream marshmallow crème, cream cheese, sugar, and vanilla in a medium bowl. Spread filling over crust. Arrange blueberries and strawberries over filling. Chill until ready to serve.

Note: Any type of fresh fruit can be used on this pie.

Fudgy Nut Pie

⅔ cup sugar
⅓ cup all-purpose flour
¼ tsp. salt
2 1-oz. squares unsweetened chocolate, melted
1¼ cups dark corn syrup
3 eggs
3 T. butter, melted
2 tsp. vanilla
½ cup chopped pecans
½ cup chopped walnuts
single piecrust, unbaked
¼ cup pecan halves
vanilla ice cream (to serve)

Preheat oven to 350°. In a large bowl, combine sugar, flour, and salt. Set aside. In a separate bowl, whisk together melted chocolate, dark corn syrup, eggs, melted butter, and vanilla. Stir into dry ingredients and beat well to combine. Fold in chopped pecans and walnuts. Pour into piecrust. Arrange pecan halves over top of pie. Bake 55 to 60 minutes. Let cool. Serve with vanilla ice cream if desired.

Funeral Pie

double piecrust, unbaked
2 cups raisins
2 cups water, divided
½ cup brown sugar
½ cup granulated sugar
3 T. cornstarch
1½ tsp. cinnamon
¼ tsp. allspice
pinch of salt
1 T. cider vinegar
3 T. butter

Line a pie pan with half the pastry and set in refrigerator to chill. Place the raisins and ⅔ cup of the water in a saucepan and heat over medium heat 5 minutes. Combine sugars, cornstarch, cinnamon, allspice, and salt in a bowl and while constantly stirring, slowly add the remaining water. Add this mixture to the heating raisins. Cook and stir until the mixture begins to bubble. Add the vinegar and butter and heat just until the butter is melted. Remove from heat and allow mixture to cool. Pour into the prepared pie shell and top with the second crust.

Bake 25 minutes at 400° or until golden. The pie will set up as it cools.

Grape Pie

4 cups red grapes
3 T. all-purpose flour
1 T. lemon juice
1 cup sugar
½ tsp. salt
2 T. butter
½ tsp. nutmeg
double piecrust, unbaked

Preheat oven to 425°. Halve grapes and cook in a medium saucepan on low heat for 5 minutes. Stir in flour, lemon juice, sugar, salt, and butter. Cook 2 minutes longer, stirring constantly. Pour mixture into unbaked piecrust. Sprinkle nutmeg over grape mixture and cover with top crust. Brush with egg wash if desired and cut several steam vents. Bake 40 to 45 minutes. Let cool completely before serving.

Green Tomato Pie

3 cups green tomatoes, peeled and chopped
2 cups green apples, peeled and chopped
2 T. lemon juice
½ cup brown sugar
1 T. all-purpose flour
½ tsp. salt
1 tsp. cinnamon
¼ tsp. cloves
¼ tsp. ginger
double piecrust, unbaked
2 T. butter, cubed

Preheat oven to 375°. In a large bowl, toss tomatoes and apples with lemon juice. Set aside. In a separate bowl, combine brown sugar, flour, salt, cinnamon, cloves, and ginger. Add to tomato mixture and toss gently to combine. Pour into an unbaked piecrust and dot with cubes of butter. Cover with top crust and brush with egg wash if desired. Bake 50 to 55 minutes. Let cool completely before serving.

Impossible Pie

4 eggs, beaten
2 cups milk

2 tsp. vanilla
¼ cup butter, melted
¾ cup sugar
1 cup all-purpose flour
2 tsp. baking powder
¾ cup coconut

Grease a pie plate well and set aside. Preheat oven to 350°. In a large bowl, combine beaten eggs, milk, vanilla, and melted butter. Set aside. In a separate bowl, combine sugar, flour, and baking powder. Add dry ingredients into egg mixture and whisk well to combine. Pour mixture into a greased pie plate and sprinkle coconut over the top. Bake 40 to 50 minutes. Let cool completely before serving.

Note: This pie forms its own crust during the baking process.

Key Lime Pie

2 eggs
2 egg whites
½ cup key lime juice
1 tsp. lime zest
1 14-oz can sweetened condensed milk
graham cracker crust
1 cup whipping cream
1 T. sugar
1 tsp. vanilla

Preheat oven to 350°. In a large bowl, beat eggs and whites until foamy. Gradually add key lime juice, lime zest, and sweetened condensed milk. Whisk until combined. Spoon into graham cracker crust. Bake 20 minutes or until almost set. (The center will set as the pie chills.) Let cool 15 minutes, then cover loosely and chill 4 hours.

Just before serving, beat whipping cream, sugar, and vanilla until stiff peaks form. Spread whipped cream over top of pie and serve.

- -

Lemon Chess Pie

1 cup sugar
¼ cup butter, softened
1 T. all-purpose flour
1 T. cornmeal
3 eggs, beaten until foamy
½ cup heavy cream
¼ cup fresh lemon juice
4 T. lemon zest
single piecrust, unbaked

Preheat oven to 350°. In a large bowl, cream sugar and butter. Add flour and cornmeal to creamed mixture and stir to combine. Slowly whisk in beaten eggs and cream until fluffy. Stir in lemon juice and lemon zest. Mix until smooth and pour into an unbaked piecrust. Bake 35 to 40 minutes or until center is just set. Let cool completely and refrigerate until ready to serve.

- -

Lemon Meringue Pie

Lemon Filling
1 cup sugar
2 T. all-purpose flour
3 T. cornstarch
¼ tsp. salt
1½ cups milk
2 tsp. vanilla
¼ cup lemon juice
zest of 2 lemons
2 T. butter

4 egg yolks, beaten
single piecrust, prebaked

Meringue
4 egg whites
6 T. sugar

Preheat oven to 350°. To make lemon filling, whisk sugar, flour, cornstarch, and salt together in a medium saucepan. Stir in milk, vanilla, lemon juice, and lemon zest. Cook over medium-high heat, stirring frequently, until mixture just comes to a boil. Stir in butter until melted. Whisk ½ cup of hot lemon mixture into beaten egg yolks. Pour egg yolk mixture into hot saucepan and whisk to combine. Return to a boil, whisking constantly, and cook until mixture begins to thicken. Remove from heat and pour filling into baked crust.

To make meringue, beat egg whites until foamy. Add sugar and whip until stiff peaks form. Spread meringue completely over lemon filling, being sure to bring it to the edges. Bake 10 minutes or until meringue begins to turn golden brown. Cool at room temperature for 1 hour and refrigerate uncovered until ready to serve.

Lime Chiffon Pie

1 package Oreo cookies
½ cup butter, melted
6 egg whites
¾ cup sugar
2 small packages lime Jell-O
½ cup boiling water
2 cups cream, whipped

Open the cookies and remove and discard the cream filling. Crush the cookies until you have fine crumbles. Stir the crushed cookies with the melted butter and then mold the cookie crust into 2 pie plates or one 9 x 13-inch glass pan, covering the bottom and sides of the pan.

Whip the egg whites until stiff peaks form. Add the sugar and beat well again. Set aside for now.

Stir together the 2 packages of lime Jell-O with ½ cup boiling water until dissolved.

Fold the Jell-O mixture into the stiffly beaten egg whites, then add the cream and mix gently but well. Spoon over the crust in the pan(s) and chill well before serving.

Maple Cream Pie

single piecrust, prebaked
1 14-oz. can sweetened condensed milk
⅔ cup maple syrup
small pinch salt
1 cup heavy cream
¼ cup powdered sugar
1 tsp. vanilla
3 T. chopped pecans

In a medium saucepan, mix together the sweetened condensed milk, maple syrup, and salt. Cook over low heat, stirring constantly, until mixture begins to boil and bubble up. Cook 4 minutes being careful that liquid doesn't scorch. Pour into a baked piecrust. Let cool completely (takes about 3 hours).

In a bowl that has been set in the refrigerator to chill beforehand, stir together the cream, powdered sugar, and vanilla. Beat until stiff peaks form. Spread on the cooled pie and top with pecans. Chill until ready to serve.

Maple Walnut Pie

⅓ cup sugar
⅓ cup brown sugar
¼ tsp. salt

6 T. butter, melted
4 eggs, lightly beaten
1 cup maple syrup
1 cup coarsely chopped walnuts
single piecrust, unbaked

Preheat oven to 400°. In a large bowl, combine sugar, brown sugar, and salt. Stir in melted butter, beaten eggs, and maple syrup. Whisk to combine. Fold in walnuts. Pour mixture into crust and bake 10 minutes. Reduce oven temperature to 325° and bake 50 minutes longer. Let cool completely before serving.

- -

Oatmeal Pie

3 egg whites
½ tsp. cream of tartar
1 cup sugar
½ cup quick-cooking rolled oats
6 saltine crackers, crushed
½ cup crushed pecans
2 tsp. vanilla
1 T. butter, cubed
dash cinnamon
dash nutmeg

Grease a pie plate and set aside. Preheat oven to 375°. In a large bowl, beat egg whites and cream of tartar until foamy. Add sugar and beat until stiff peaks form. Fold in oats, crushed saltines, crushed pecans, and vanilla. Pour mixture into a greased pie plate and dot with cubes of butter. Sprinkle with cinnamon and nutmeg. Bake 25 to 30 minutes. Let cool completely before serving.

Note: This pie forms its own crust during the baking process.

PIES, COBBLERS, AND CRISPS

Peach Pie

1¼ cups sugar
⅓ cup all-purpose flour
½ tsp. cinnamon
¼ tsp. nutmeg
1 T. lemon juice
4 cups peaches, peeled and sliced
2 T. butter, cubed
double piecrust, unbaked

Preheat oven to 375°. Combine sugar, flour, cinnamon, and nutmeg in a large bowl. Add lemon juice and peaches. Toss gently to combine and let rest 10 minutes for juices to distribute. Pour peaches into unbaked pie shell and dot with cubes of butter. Cover with top crust and brush with egg wash if desired. Cut steam vents. Bake 40 to 50 minutes until juices are beginning to bubble and crust is golden brown. Let cool completely before serving.

Peanut Butter Pie

2 eggs, separated
¾ cup sugar
⅓ cup creamy peanut butter
½ cup milk
1 tsp. vanilla
¼ tsp. salt
single piecrust, unbaked
whipped cream (to serve)

Preheat oven to 375°. In a large bowl, beat egg yolks until lemon-colored. Beat in sugar until combined. Blend in peanut butter. Slowly beat in milk, vanilla, and salt. Set aside. In a separate bowl, whip egg whites until stiff peaks form. Fold egg whites into peanut butter mixture. Pour into crust and bake 30 to 35 minutes. Let cool. Top with whipped cream before serving.

Pear Pie

3 T. unflavored gelatin
¾ cup sugar
¼ tsp. salt
½ tsp. ginger
½ tsp. cinnamon
¼ tsp. nutmeg
3 eggs, separated
5 cups pears, peeled, cored, and sliced
¼ tsp. cream of tartar
Gingersnap Crust
1 cup heavy cream

In a medium saucepan, combine gelatin, sugar, salt, ginger, cinnamon, and nutmeg. Set aside. In a separate bowl, beat egg yolks until just foamy. Stir egg yolks into sugar mixture. Bring to a boil over low heat, stirring constantly. Add pears and toss gently to combine. Cook 3 minutes longer, stirring occasionally. Remove from heat and let cool. Chill in refrigerator 1 hour.

Beat egg whites and cream of tartar until whites form stiff peaks. Fold beaten whites into pear mixture and pour into Gingersnap Crust. Set aside. In a separate bowl, whip heavy cream until soft peaks form. Spread whipped cream over pie filling. Garnish with a dash of nutmeg, if desired.

Pecan Pie

1¼ cups sugar
¼ cup dark corn syrup
¼ cup butter
2 tsp. cornstarch
1 T. cold water
3 eggs
¼ tsp. salt
2 tsp. vanilla
2 cups chopped pecans
single piecrust, unbaked

Preheat oven to 400°. In a saucepan, combine sugar, corn syrup, and butter. Mix cornstarch and water in a small bowl and add to saucepan. Bring to a rolling boil, stirring frequently, and remove from heat. Set aside.

In a large bowl, beat eggs just until frothy and gradually whisk in the syrup mixture. Add salt and vanilla and stir to combine. Fold in pecans and pour into piecrust. Bake 15 minutes. Reduce oven temperature to 325° and bake 25 to 30 minutes longer or until filling is set. Let cool completely before serving.

Note: Maple syrup can be substituted for dark corn syrup if desired.

Peppermint Party Pie

2 cups (about 24) crushed Oreos
¼ cup butter, melted
¼ cup milk
7-oz. jar marshmallow crème
1 tsp. vanilla
1½ cups whipped cream
½ cup crushed peppermint candy
1 oz. semisweet chocolate, melted

In a medium bowl, combine crushed Oreos and melted butter. Press into bottom of a 9-inch pie plate and chill until firm.

In a large bowl, mix together milk and marshmallow crème until well blended. Stir in vanilla and then fold in whipped cream and peppermint candy. Spoon into chilled crust and drizzle with melted chocolate. Cut through filling with a knife to create a marbled effect. Freeze pie until firm, at least 3 hours.

- -

Plum Crisp

12 plums, pitted and chopped
1 cup sugar, divided
1 cup all-purpose flour
1½ tsp. baking powder
1 tsp. salt
1 egg, beaten
1 tsp. vanilla
½ cup butter, melted
vanilla ice cream, to serve

Preheat oven to 350°. Grease an 8-inch square baking dish and place chopped plums in the bottom. Sprinkle with ¼ cup sugar and set aside. In a medium bowl, mix together remaining ¾ cup sugar, flour, baking powder, and salt. Mix in beaten egg and vanilla. Spoon mixture over plums. Drizzle with melted butter and bake 40 minutes or until golden. Serve warm over vanilla ice cream.

Pumpkin Pie

1½ cups or 1 15-oz. can pumpkin
1 T. butter, melted
½ cup brown sugar
¼ cup sugar
½ tsp. salt
1 tsp. cinnamon
¼ tsp. nutmeg
¼ tsp. ginger
⅛ tsp. allspice
⅛ tsp. cloves
1 T. all-purpose flour
2 eggs
1 T. molasses
1 tsp. vanilla
2 cups milk
single piecrust, unbaked

Preheat oven to 450°. In a large bowl, combine pumpkin, butter, brown sugar, sugar, salt, cinnamon, nutmeg, ginger, allspice, cloves, and flour. Mix well. Beat in eggs, molasses, and vanilla. Slowly whisk in milk. Pour mixture into crust. Bake 10 minutes. Reduce temperature to 350° and bake 90 minutes longer. Let cool completely before serving.

Raisin Walnut Pie

2 cups raisins
1 cup boiling water
3 eggs
½ cup brown sugar
½ tsp. salt
½ tsp. cinnamon
¼ tsp. nutmeg
¼ tsp. cloves
⅓ cup butter, melted

½ cup maple syrup
½ cup chopped walnuts
double piecrust, unbaked

Preheat oven to 425°. Place raisins in a large, heatproof bowl and pour boiling water over top. Stir to combine and let stand 5 minutes to hydrate. Beat eggs in a separate bowl and whisk in brown sugar, salt, cinnamon, nutmeg, and cloves. Stir in melted butter and maple syrup. Pour mixture over raisins and stir to combine. Fold in walnuts. Pour over piecrust. Cover with top crust and brush with egg wash if desired. Cut steam vents and bake 20 to 25 minutes or until crust is golden brown.

Raspberry Pie

1¼ cups sugar
3 scant T. cornstarch
2 T. quick-cooking tapioca
2 T. lemon juice
zest of half a lemon
1 qt. fresh raspberries
2 T. butter, cubed
double piecrust, unbaked

Preheat oven to 425°. In a large bowl, combine sugar, cornstarch, and tapioca. Add lemon juice, lemon zest, and raspberries and toss gently to combine. Let stand 30 minutes for juices to distribute. Pour raspberries into piecrust and dot with small cubes of butter. Cover with top crust and cut steam vents. Bake 15 minutes. Reduce oven temperature to 350° and bake 35 to 40 minutes longer. Let cool completely before serving.

PIES, COBBLERS, AND CRISPS

Rhubarb Crisp

Rhubarb Filling
4 cups rhubarb, chopped into ½-inch pieces
1½ cups sugar

Batter
½ cup butter
⅓ cup sugar
2 tsp. baking powder
½ tsp. salt
¼ tsp. nutmeg
1 T. vanilla
1 tsp. orange zest
1 cup all-purpose flour
½ cup milk

Topping
¼ cup sugar
2 T. cornstarch
½ cup boiling water

Preheat oven to 375°. To make rhubarb filling, combine chopped rhubarb and sugar in a large bowl. Pour into a greased 9 x 13-inch baking dish.

To make batter, cream butter and sugar in a large bowl. Stir in baking powder, salt, nutmeg, vanilla, orange zest, and flour. Whisk in milk until well combined. Pour batter over rhubarb.

To make topping, combine sugar and cornstarch in a small bowl. Sprinkle over batter. Pour boiling water over top. Bake 40 minutes or until topping is golden brown. Serve warm.

Rhubarb Custard Pie

3 eggs
3 T. milk

2 cups sugar
3 T. quick-cooking tapioca
4 cups diced rhubarb, fresh or frozen (thaw before
    using)
double piecrust, unbaked
2 tsp. butter
cinnamon sugar for sprinkling (optional)

Preheat oven to 400°. In a medium bowl, lightly beat the eggs. Blend in milk. In a separate bowl, combine the sugar and tapioca and then stir into the egg mixture. Let set for 15 minutes.

Pour rhubarb into piecrust and then pour egg mixture over rhubarb. Dot with butter. Cover with top crust. Cut a cross into the top crust to vent steam while pie is baking. Bake 15 minutes. Reduce heat to 350° and bake an additional 35 to 40 minutes. Remove the pie from the oven and sprinkle with cinnamon sugar if desired.

Rhubarb Pie

1¼ cups sugar
¼ cup all-purpose flour
¼ tsp. salt
4 cups rhubarb, cut into ½-inch pieces
zest of 1 lemon
1 T. lemon juice
double piecrust, unbaked
1 T. butter, cubed
¼ tsp. nutmeg

Preheat oven to 350°. Combine sugar, flour, and salt in a large bowl. Add chopped rhubarb, lemon zest, and lemon juice and toss to combine. Let stand 15 minutes for juices to distribute. Pour rhubarb mixture into piecrust. Dot with cubed butter and sprinkle with nutmeg. Cover with top crust and brush with egg wash if desired. Cut steam vents and bake 50 to 60 minutes or until juices begin to bubble and crust is golden. Let cool completely before serving.

Shoofly Pie

¾ cup molasses
½ cup hot water
¾ tsp. baking soda
1 egg, lightly beaten
1½ cups all-purpose flour
¾ cup brown sugar
¼ cup shortening
single piecrust, unbaked

Preheat oven to 400°. In a medium bowl, combine molasses, hot water, and baking soda. Whisk in beaten egg. Set aside. In a separate bowl, combine flour and brown sugar. Using a pastry blender, cut in shortening until mixture resembles coarse crumbs.

Pour half of molasses mixture into piecrust. Sprinkle half of crumb mixture over top. Pour remaining molasses mixture over crumbs and finish with remaining crumb mixture. Bake 15 minutes. Reduce oven temperature to 350° and bake an additional 30 minutes. Let cool 30 minutes before serving. This pie is best served warm.

Strawberry Pie

1 cup sugar
½ cup all-purpose flour
pinch of salt
5 cups sliced strawberries
2 T. butter, cut in cubes
double piecrust, unbaked

Preheat oven to 425°. Combine sugar, flour, and salt in a medium bowl. Add sliced strawberries and toss lightly to combine. Spread in pie shell and dot with cubes of butter. Top with second crust and brush lightly with egg wash if desired. Cut vents in top crust and bake 35 to 45 minutes or until juices begin to bubble and crust is golden brown. Let cool completely before serving.

Strawberry Rhubarb Pie

1 cup sugar
½ cup all-purpose flour
3-4 cups rhubarb, chopped
1 qt. chopped strawberries
2 T. butter, cubed
double piecrust, unbaked

In a large bowl, whisk together sugar and flour. Add rhubarb and strawberries and toss to combine. Let stand 30 minutes to distribute juices.

Preheat oven to 400°. Pour filling into crust and dot with chopped butter. Cover pie with top crust and brush with egg wash and a pinch of sugar if desired. Cut steam vents in top crust. Bake 35 to 40 minutes or until juices bubble and crust is golden brown. Let cool completely before serving.

Sweet Potato Pie

1 lb. sweet potatoes, cooked, peeled, and mashed
3 eggs, separated
½ cup heavy cream
½ cup brown sugar
2 T. butter, melted
1 tsp. vanilla
1 tsp. allspice
¼ tsp. nutmeg
dash of salt
single piecrust, unbaked

Preheat oven to 400°. In a large bowl, combine mashed sweet potatoes, egg yolks, heavy cream, brown sugar, butter, vanilla, allspice, nutmeg, and salt. Mix well. In a separate bowl, beat egg whites until soft peaks form. Fold egg whites into sweet potato mixture. Pour mixture into crust and bake 40 to 45 minutes or until a knife inserted into the center comes out clean. Let cool completely before serving.

Vinegar Pie

2 cups water
½ cup all-purpose flour
2 cups sugar
2 eggs, beaten until frothy
6 T. apple cider vinegar
2 tsp. lemon juice
single piecrust, prebaked

Boil water in a medium saucepan. In a small bowl, combine flour and sugar. Add mixture to boiling water and cook, stirring frequently, until thickened, 5 to 7 minutes. Remove from heat and add the eggs slowly, whisking constantly. Return to medium-low heat and cook, stirring, until thickened and smooth, about 3 minutes. Remove from heat and stir in the apple cider vinegar and lemon juice. Pour through a fine-mesh strainer to remove any lumps. Pour mixture into prebaked piecrust and chill until set, at least 4 hours.

INDEX

Yeast Breads

Cornell University's Triple-Rich Protein
   Formula 15
Basic Per Loaf Bread 19
Basic White Bread 20
Black Bread 21
Cheddar Cheese Bread 22
Cinnamon Raisin Bread 23
Dilly Rye Bread 24
Egg Bread 26
French Bread 27
German Dark Rye Bread 29
Honey Oatmeal Bread 30
Oatmeal Bread 31

Peasant Bread 32
Potato Bread 32
Raisin Oatmeal Bread 33
Round Rye Bread 34
Sour Cream Dill Bread 35
Sunflower Flax Seed Bread 36
Three Flours Bread 37
Walnut Bread 38
Wheat Bread 39
Wheat Bread—Large Batch 40
White Bread 41
Whole Wheat Milk Bread 42
100% Whole Wheat Bread 43

- -

Bagels, Buns, Pizza Crusts, and More

Bagels

Basic Bagels 46
Blueberry Bagels 47
Cheese and Jalapeño Bagels 47
Cinnamon Raisin Bagels 49
Everything Bagels 50

- - - - -

Crackers

Graham Crackers 50

Oliver Oil and Sesame Seed Crackers 51
Soda Crackers 51
Whole Wheat Crackers 52

- - - - -

English Muffins

Cinnamon Raisin English Muffins 53
Oven Baked Wheat English Muffins 54
Plain English Muffins 55

- - - - -

Pretzels

Soft Pretzels 56
Yeast-Free Soft Pretzels 57

- - - - -

Pizza Crust and Dinner Rolls

Dinner Rolls 58
Hamburger or Hot Dog Buns 59
Hoagie Sandwich Rolls 60

Jiffy Pizza Crust 61
Mashed Potato Rolls 61
Overnight Butterhorns 62
Overnight No-Knead Butter Rolls 63
Pizza Crust 64
Quick and Easy Pizza Crust 65
Quick Cloverleaf Rolls 65
Rachael's Cracked Wheat Potato Rolls 66
Refrigerator Dinner Rolls 67

Quick Breads

Apple Pecan Bread 70
Applesauce Nut Bread 70
Banana Nut Bread 71
Carrot Bread 72
Carrot Pineapple Bread 72
Chocolate Zucchini Bread 73
Communion Bread (Unleavened) 74
Corn Bread 74
Corn Bread with Cheese and Bacon 75
Dutch Apple Bread 76
Garlic Cheese Breadsticks 76
Ginger Pumpkin Bread 77

Green Chili Cheese Bread 78
Hawaiian Bread 78
Lemon Bread 79
Lemon Walnut Bread 80
Onion Cheese Bread 81
Orange Nut Bread 82
Peanut Butter Bread 82
Pumpkin Bread 83
Sour Cream Corn Bread 84
Walnut Bread with Streusel Filling 84
Whole Wheat Quick Buttermilk Bread 85
Zucchini Bread 85

Biscuits and Muffins

Angel Biscuits 88
Buttermilk Biscuits 88
Cheesy Biscuits 89
Cream Scones 90
Crisp Biscuits 91
Drop Biscuits 91
Herb Biscuits 92
Lard Biscuits 92
Light and Airy Biscuits 93
Popovers 93
Savory Potato and Vegetable Scones 94
Traditional Biscuits 95

- - - - -

Bacon and Cheddar Cheese Muffins 96
Berry Muffins 96

Blueberry Oatmeal Muffins 97
Bread Crumb Muffins 98
Chocolate Chip Muffins 98
Cornmeal Muffins 99
Four-Week Refrigerator Bran Muffins 99
Fresh Peach Muffins 100
Ginger Muffins 101
Graham Muffins 101
Lemon Muffins 102
Oatmeal Muffins 102
Sour Cream Muffins 103
Whole Wheat Muffins 103
Whole Wheat Pineapple Muffins 104

Doughnuts and Sweet Rolls

Apple Fritters 107
Bismarcks 107
Blackberry Cheese Roll 108
Caramel Apple Dumplings 109
Chocolate Baking Powder Doughnuts 110
Cinnamon Fans 111
Cinnamon Rolls 112
Cream Sticks 113
Doughnuts for a Crowd 114
Easy Cinnamon Rolls 115
Fastnachts 116
Fattigman 117
German Rolls 118
Glazed Doughnuts 119

Jelly Doughnuts 120
Knee Patches 121
Long Johns 122
Maple Bars 123
Moist Doughnuts 124
Old-Fashioned Sour Cream
    Doughnuts 125
Oven-Baked Doughnuts 127
Pecan Caramel Rolls 128
Pluckems 129
Quick Sticky Buns 130
Rhubarb Dumplings 132
Soft Sugar Doughnuts 133
Sour Cream Buttermilk Doughnuts 134

Cookies

Amish Nut Balls 138
Apple Butter Cookies 138
Applesauce Cookies 139
Brown Sugar Freezer Cookies 139
Caramel Chocolate Cookies 140
Chocolate Cookies 141
Chocolate Chip Cookies 141
Chocolate Crinkle Cookies 142
Cranberry Shortbread Cookies 142
Cream Cheese Snowballs 143
Date and Walnut Drops 144
Gingersnaps 144
Grasshopper Cookies 145
Jam-Filled Butter Cookies 146
Lemon Pudding Cookies 147
M&M Cookies 147
Maple Cookies 148
Marshmallow-Peanut Crisps 148
Molasses Crinkles 149
Monster Cookies 150
Oatmeal Cookies 150
Oatmeal Coconut Cookies 151

Oatmeal Raisin Cookies 152
Peanut Butter Cookies 152
Peppermint Sugar Cookies 153
Pralines 154
Pumpkin Cookies 154
Sand Tarts 155
Shortbread Cookies 156
Snickerdoodles 156
Soft Molasses Cookies 157
Sugar Cookies 158
White Chocolate Chip Cookies 158
White Chocolate Macadamia Nut
    Cookies 159

Bars

Almond Bars 162
Apple Butter Bars 162
Apple Butterscotch Bars 163
Apricot Date Bars 164
Banana Date Bars 164
Blondies 165
Blueberry Shortbread Bars 166
Brownies 166
Caramel Bars 167
Cheesecake Bars 168
Cheesecake Blondies 169
Cherry Pie Bars 170
Chewy Granola Bars 170
Chocolate Orange Bars 171
Chocolate Peanut Butter Bars 172
Cinnamon Bars 172
Cinnamon Coffee Bars 173

Coconut Bars 174
Cranberry Bars 175
Crispy Chocolate Crackles 176
Date Nut Squares 176
Dream Bars 177
Gooey Nut Squares 177
Granola Bars 178
Lemon Bars 179
Lemon Blondies 180
Lemon Cheesecake Bars 180
Peanut Butter Oatmeal Bars 181
Peanut Butter Brownies 182
Peanut Butter Crispies 183
Pumpkin Bars 183
Pumpkin Ice Cream Bars 184
S'mores Bars 185
Zucchini Nut Squares 185

Cakes

Angel Food Cake 188
Apple Butter Cake 189
Apple Cake 190
Apple Caramel Cake 190
Banana Nut Cake 192
Blueberry Cake 192
Blueberry Streusel Cake 193
Buttermilk Coffee Cake with Crumb
    Topping 194
Carrot Cake 195
Cherry Coffee Cake 196
Chocolate Applesauce Cake 196
Chocolate Cake 197
Chocolate Chiffon Cake 198
Christmas Cake 199
Coffee Cake 199
Crumb Cake 200
Fresh Apple Cake 201
Fudge Cake 202
German Oat Cake 202

Gingerbread Cake 203
Gold Cake 204
Half-Pound Cake 204
Holiday Gift Cake 205
Mocha Pudding Cake 206
Nutmeg Cake 206
Oatmeal Cake 207
Orange Loaf Cake 208
Peach Coffee Cake 209
Peach-Filled Coffee Cake 210
Pineapple Cake 211
Pound Cake 211
Pumpkin Cake 212
Rhubarb Coffee Cake 213
Salad Dressing Chocolate Cake 214
Slush Cake 214
Spice Cake 215
Sponge Cake 216
Tunnel of Fudge Cake 216
Two-Egg Cake 217

Walnut Cake 218
White Fruit Cake 218

Yellow Cake 219

- -

Pies, Cobblers, and Crisps

Crusts

Best Piecrust 222
Gingersnap Crust 222
Graham Cracker Crust 223
Prebaked Piecrust 223

- - - - -

Pies, Cobblers, and Crisps

Apple Crisp 224
Apple Crumb Pie 225
Apple Pear Crumble 226
Apple Pie 226
Apple Turnovers 227
Apricot Pie 229
Banana Cream Pie 229
Black Raspberry Cobbler 230
Blackberry Cobbler 231
Blueberry Pie 232
Bob and Andy Pie 232
Brown Sugar Pie 233
Buttermilk Pie 234
Butterscotch Pie 234
Caramel Apple Pie 235
Carrot Pie 236
Cheesecake 237
Cherry Cobbler 238
Cherry-Rhubarb Pie 238
Chocolate Pie 239
Chocolate Strawberry Pie 240
Cranberry Walnut Pie 240
Currant Pie 241
Custard Pie 242

Dutch Apple Pie 242
Fourth of July Berry Pie 243
Fudgy Nut Pie 244
Funeral Pie 245
Grape Pie 245
Green Tomato Pie 246
Impossible Pie 246
Key Lime Pie 247
Lemon Chess Pie 248
Lemon Meringue Pie 248
Lime Chiffon Pie 249
Maple Cream Pie 250
Maple Walnut Pie 250
Oatmeal Pie 251
Peach Pie 252
Peanut Butter Pie 252
Pear Pie 253
Pecan Pie 254
Peppermint Party Pie 254
Plum Crisp 255
Pumpkin Pie 256
Raisin Walnut Pie 256
Raspberry Pie 257
Rhubarb Crisp 258
Rhubarb Custard Pie 258
Rhubarb Pie 259
Shoofly Pie 260
Strawberry Pie 260
Strawberry Rhubarb Pie 261
Sweet Potato Pie 261
Vinegar Pie 262

About the Authors

Georgia Varozza, author of *The Homestyle Amish Kitchen Cookbook* (more than 60,000 copies sold), is a certified master food preserver. She teaches people how to prepare and preserve healthy foods, live simply with integrity, and get the most from what they have. She works in publishing and lives in a small Oregon community. Georgia loves being with her kids and grandkids and enjoys cooking, spinning, and knitting. Visit Georgia at www.georgiaplainandsimple.blogspot.com.

Kathleen Kerr grew up around books, and when she got old enough she decided to try making them herself. She works in publishing and is a frequent speaker at conferences around the country. Kathleen lives with her husband and daughter in the Pacific Northwest, where she can often be found hiking, writing, and creating chaos in the kitchen. Visit her at www.quillsandquiche.blogspot.com.

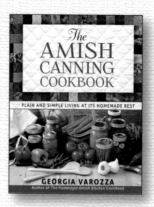

The Amish Canning Cookbook

By Georgia Varozza

From the author of *The Homestyle Amish Kitchen Cookbook* comes a great new collection of recipes, hints, and Plain wisdom for everyone who loves the idea of preserving fresh, wholesome foods. Whether instructing a beginning canner or helping a seasoned cook hone her skills, certified master food preserver Georgia Varozza shows people how to get the very best out of their food. Here, readers will find...

- a short history of canning
- lists of all the tools and supplies needed to get started
- basic instructions for safe canning
- recipes for canning fruit, vegetables, meat, soups, sauces, and more
- guidelines for adapting recipes to fit personal tastes

With its expert advice and warm tones, *The Amish Canning Cookbook* will become a beloved companion to those who love the tradition, frugality, and homestyle flavor of Amish cooking!

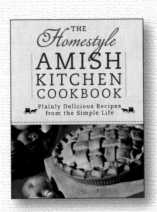

The Homestyle Amish Kitchen Cookbook

By Georgia Varozza

Just about everyone is fascinated by the Amish—their simple, family-centered lifestyle, colorful quilts, and hearty, homemade meals. Straight from the heart of Amish country, this celebration of hearth and home will delight readers with the pleasures of the family table as they take a peek at the Amish way of life—a life filled with the self-reliance and peace of mind that many of us long for.

Readers will appreciate the scores of tasty, easy-to-prepare recipes such as Scrapple, Graham "Nuts" Cereal, Potato Rivvel Soup, Amish Dressing, and Snitz Pie. At the same time they'll learn a bit about the Amish, savor interesting tidbits from the "Amish Kitchen Wisdom" sections, find out just how much food it takes to feed the large number of folks attending preaching services, barn raisings, weddings, and work frolics, and much more.

The Homestyle Amish Kitchen Cookbook is filled with good, old-fashioned family meal ideas to help bring the simple life home!

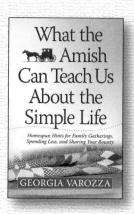

What the Amish Can Teach Us About the Simple Life

By Georgia Varozza

Emphasizing Amish values of faith, simplicity, and self-sufficiency, author Georgia Varozza (*The Homestyle Amish Kitchen Cookbook*) offers fresh ideas to make faith, serenity, and healthy living a stronger presence in everyday life. Drawing on her family's Plain roots, she provides innovative suggestions and easy-to-follow instructions to help readers

- create a home atmosphere that promotes faith and family
- simplify their lives by controlling technology
- enjoy the satisfaction of successful do-it-yourself projects
- discover the benefits of growing and raising their own food
- generate less waste by repurposing, reusing, and recycling

Practical and hands-on, this book is a great resource for people who want to make a few simple changes or fully embrace a more wholesome lifestyle.